Introduction

"I realized very early the power of food to evoke memory, to bring people together, to transport you to other places, and I wanted to be a part of that."
– José Andrés Puerta

One of my favorite things about traveling is the food. The adventure of eating something new is almost as exciting as seeing something new! When my husband and I
settled down to start our family, I knew I would have to put traveling on hold for the foreseeable future. As amazing and adventurous as motherhood was, I was going to miss traveling.
After my second was born, I decided I wanted to put together a series of recipes from all over the world. I wanted myself and others to be able travel and explore new foods, without leaving our homes.
My goal with this book was to help craft and create recipes from 80 different countries, and make them easy enough to make in your own kitchen with minimal new tools and equipment. (Being able to make a fresh chimney cake in your own oven is one of my favorite feats to date!) While it was challenging, it was very rewarding! My children and my husband (Bless him for being my guinea pig) got to enjoy some of my favorite foods from all over the globe.
Despite all the trials and many errors, I was able to make a cookbook that brings international food to your kitchen.
I hope you enjoy these recipes as much as I do, and that it inspires you to make your own memories and have your own adventures with your family.

Kyleigh Jackson

Traveling back to Indiana after a trip to Panama

Small village in Volcán
Chiriquí Province, Panama

Hungarian Parliament Visitor Centre
Országház Látogatóközpont

Countries

Afghanistan	Jamaica	Uruguay
Argentina	Japan	USA
Australia	Laos	Venezuela
Bahamas	Latvia	Vietnam
Bolivia	Libya	Zimbabwe
Brazil	Madagascar	
Bulgaria	Malaysia	
Burma	Marshall Island	
Cambodia	Mexico	
Canada	Morocco	
Chile	Nepal	
China	Netherlands	
Columbia	New Zealand	
Costa Rica	Nicaragua	
Croatia	Nigeria	
Cuba	Norway	
Denmark	Pakistan	
Dominican Republic	Panama	
Ecuador	Peru	
Egypt	Philippines	
El Salvador	Poland	
Ethiopia	Portugal	
Fiji	Romania	
Finland	Russia	
France	Samoa	
Germany	Serbia	
Greece	Singapore	
Guatemala	South Africa	
Honduras	South Korea	
Hungary	Spain	
Iceland	Switzerland	
India	Taiwan	
Indonesia	Thailand	
Iran	Turkey	
Ireland	Uganda	
Israel	Ukraine	
Italy	United Kingdom	

Country: Afghanistan   **Servings: 6**

INGREDIENTS:

For the dough:
- 3 ½ C all-purpose flour
- 1 Tsp salt • 2 Tbs oil
- 1¼ C water

For the filling:
- 1½ lbs potatoes
- 2 C packed sliced green onion
- 2 C packed cilantro
- ½ C chopped green pepper or to taste
- 1 Tsp black pepper
- 1 Tsp salt or to taste
- 2 Tbs olive oil
- Additional oil for shallow frying

Serve with Lubia Polo on page 74

INSTRUCTIONS:

For the dough: 1.Combine flour, salt, and oil in the bowl of a food processor. With the motor running, add water until the dough comes together in a ball. It should not be too sticky or too dry. 2.Remove the dough from the processor and give it a couple of kneads on the counter. Wrap in plastic and let rest about 20 minutes.

For the filling: 1.Wash potatoes, prick with a fork, and microwave until soft, approximately 10 minutes depending on the size of your potatoes. Potatoes are done when you can easily pierce them with a knife and they feel soft. 2.When the potatoes are finished and cool enough to handle, remove the skins and coarsely mash with a fork. 3.Roughly chop the cilantro. 3.In a skillet, heat olive oil. 4.Sauté green pepper for 1 minute. 5.Add green onion and sauté for 2 minutes. 6.Turn off the heat and stir in chopped cilantro, salt, and pepper. 7.Gently stir in the potatoes.

To form the bolani: 1. Divide the dough into 8 equal pieces and roll into balls. Keep them covered on the counter while you roll them out. 2.Divide the filling into 8 equal portions. • Roll out a ball of dough on a lightly floured surface to a 8-9 inch circle. 3.Put a portion of filling on the top half of the circle, leaving a half inch border around the edges. 4.Fold the bottom half up over the top half and seal the edges, pressing firmly all around the edge to seal it shut. 5. Repeat with the remaining balls of dough.

To shallow fry: 1.Heat 2 tablespoons oil in a large skillet on medium high. 2.One by one, shallow fry the bolani one one side until golden brown. Flip and fry on the other side til golden brown. Press down gently on the edges of the bolani while cooking to ensure that they brown evenly. 3.Place cooked bolani on a metal cooling rack while the others finish to stay crispy.

Country: Argentina   **Servings: 6**

INGREDIENTS:

Dough:
- ¾ C water, lukewarm
- ¼ C milk, lukewarm
- 2½ Tsp active dry yeast
- 2¾ C bread flour
- 2 Tsp sugar
- 1 Tsp salt
- 1 Tbs extra virgin olive oil, plus more for greasing bowl

Filling and Topping:
- 2 Tbs extra virgin olive oil, plus more for greasing and drizzling
- 2 medium onions, thinly sliced
- 1 Tsp dried oregano
- Salt to taste
- Crushed red pepper flakes to taste
- 1 lbs mozzarella cheese, grated, divided

Be sure to add plenty of cheese in the middle!

INSTRUCTIONS:

1. In a small bowl, combine water and milk. Sprinkle with yeast. Let sit for a minute before stirring to combine. Let sit until frothy, about 10 minutes.

2. In the bowl of a large food processor fitted with a dough blade or a large bowl, combine flour, sugar, and salt. Mix in the olive oil and frothy yeast with liquid until dough comes together. On a lightly floured surface, knead dough until smooth and elastic. Lightly oil a large bowl and add dough, turning to coat. Cover and let rest until doubled, about 1 hour.

3. In a large skillet, drizzle olive oil over medium heat. Thinly slice onions and add them to the pan. Cook, stirring occasionally, until softened but not brown. Stir in oregano, salt, and crushed red pepper. Remove from heat.

4. Preheat oven to 450°F. Grease a rimmed 9×13 inch pan thoroughly with olive oil.

5. Divide the dough into 2 separate pieces, one slightly larger than the other. Stretch the larger dough into a rectangle, about 8×12 inches, and place in prepared pan.

6. Evenly cover with mozzarella cheese, reserving about 1/2 cup for topping pizza, and leave a 1/2-1 inch border around the edges. Stretch the smaller piece of dough into a rectangle and place over cheese. Fold the edges of the bottom rectangle over the top rectangle and pinch to seal in the cheese.

7. Prick the top all over with a fork. Evenly top with onions and sprinkle with remaining mozzarella cheese. Lightly drizzle with olive oil.

8. Bake in preheated oven until crust is golden and top layer of cheese is bubbly and browned, about 20 minutes.

Country: Australia

Servings: 6

INGREDIENTS:
- 6 Tbs butter
- ¼ C sugar
- 2 Tbs honey generous tablespoons
- 4 C cornflakes

Honey Joys are the Australian version of Rice Krispy Treats.

INSTRUCTIONS:
1. Preheat oven to 300°F
2. Prepare 24 muffin tins lined with small paper muffin liners.
3. In a large saucepan, melt butter, sugar and honey together until frothy.
4. Add cornflakes to the hot butter mixture and mix until coated.
5. Quickly spoon into prepared muffin tins and bake for 10 minutes.

Country: Bahamas   **Servings: 2**

INGREDIENTS:
- 1 box Penne pasta
- ½ C lime juice
- ½ C dry white wine
- 1 ½ C fresh pineapple chunks
- 1 C chopped fresh mango
- ½ C chopped green onions
- ½ C chopped fresh cilantro
- 2 mahi-mahi or grouper fillets
- 4 Tbs olive oil
- 2 small Thai red hot peppers
or jalapeño peppers
- 4 clove garlic
- 1 can black beans
- Chopped cilantro

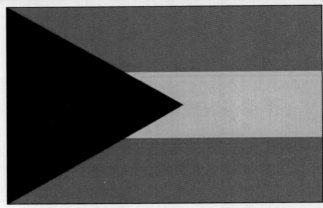

Mahi Mahi is found in the freezer section at most stores.

INSTRUCTIONS:
SALSA:
1. For salsa, place lime juice, wine, 1 cup pineapple, 1/2 cup mango, green onions, and cilantro in bowl of food processor or blender container. Pulse to coarsely chop and blend.
2. Wash mahi-mahi fillets; pat dry. Place 1/2 cup salsa in glass dish (or food-safe plastic bag); reserve remaining salsa. Add fish; turn to coat with salsa. Refrigerate, covered, 30 minutes.

FISH/PASTA:
1. Cook pasta according to package directions. Drain and return to pan.
2. Heat oil in large nonstick skillet over medium-high heat until hot. Add peppers and garlic; cook until sizzling, about 1 minute. Remove fish from salsa; pat dry. Place fish in skillet. Cook about 2 minutes until browned; turn and cook 2 minutes to sear on both sides. (Reduce heat if browning too quickly.) Pour reserved salsa around fish. Continue cooking 4 minutes or until cooked through (fish flakes easily when tested with fork).
3. Remove fish from skillet; set aside. Add beans to skillet; cook until sauce is desired consistency, stirring occasionally. Remove from heat.
4. Add pasta to skillet; toss to combine. Add remaining pineapple and mango; toss to combine. Place fish on pasta; sprinkle with cilantro, if desired.

Country: Bolivia   **Servings: 6**

INGREDIENTS:
- 2 C short-grain rice
- 1½ C crumbled queso fresco
- 1 Tbs garlic, minced
- 1 Tbs red onion, minced
- 1 C milk
- 6 C water
- salt

Use Short grain rice for a better texture.

INSTRUCTIONS:

1. Boil the water with the salt, then add the rice and keep boiling, uncovered, until almost all of the water has been absorbed or cooked off. The rice should still be pretty wet, but without pools of water and not fluffy.

2. Meanwhile, saute the garlic and onions in a small amount of oil for four or five minutes. Take care not to let them brown.

3. When the rice is nearly ready, bring the milk to a boil (warning, milk scalds easily so don't take your eyes off of it).

4. Add the milk, cheese and onion/garlic mixture to the rice. Cook over low heat, stirring, until all the cheese has melted.

Country: Brazil

Servings: 12

INGREDIENTS:
• 1 Tbs butter
• 14 oz sweetened condensed milk
• ¼ C cocoa powder
• 1 C chocolate sprinkles or shredded coconut, as needed

Classic Brigederios use chocolate sprinkles, but you can also roll in coconut!

INSTRUCTIONS:

1. In a pot over low heat, melt the butter, condensed milk, and cocoa powder, stirring continuously until you can see the bottom of the pot for 2-3 seconds when dragging a spatula through.
2. Pour onto a greased plate, then chill for 1 hour.
3. Shape and roll the chilled mixture into balls.
4. Roll the balls in chocolate sprinkles or shredded coconut.

Country: Bulgaria   **Servings: 6**

INGREDIENTS:

• 16 sheets phyllo dough, thawed
• 2 C feta cheese
• 3 large eggs
• 1 teaspoon salt
• ¾ C butter (melted)
• 1 C milk

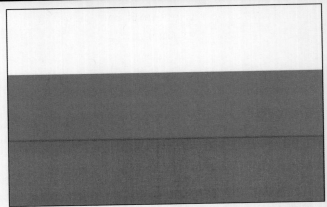

Make sure to grab phyllo dough and not pastry!

INSTRUCTIONS:

1. Preheat oven to 350°F, brush melted butter all over bottom and sides of baking pan.
2. Mix salt, cheese and milk and eggs in a bowl , combine and stir ingredients well.
3. Put down 5 sheets of phyllo dough down in buttered pan and brush over with melted butter. You can also put down one sheet at a time and butter separately.
4. Pour enough of the mixture to cover phyllo sheets and top with 3 more sheets.
5. Continue to repeat the process: put down 3 sheets and make sure to brush them well with butter then layer with mixture until all of the mixture is done, then cover with at least 2 sheets. I prefer not to butter the top sheets as they tend to get very hard after the banitsa is done baking.
6. Bake for 25-35 minutes or until golden, make sure mixture is cooked in the middle by cutting into banitsa. When the mixture is cooked it will not be runny.
7. Once banitsa is done cover it with either a towel or the lid to the pan and let it sit and cool before cutting it or serving. Covering it lets the steam soften the phyllo dough sheets.

Country: Burma/ Myanmar   **Servings: 6**

INGREDIENTS:
- 1 C fine semolina
- 1 C caster sugar
- 3 C coconut cream
- 4 Tbs clarified butter (or unsalted butter), melted
- 4 eggs
- 1 pinch of salt
- ½ Tsp ground cardamom

For the garnishing:
- 2 Tbs golden sesame seeds

Semolina is perfect for pasta making.

INSTRUCTIONS:
1. Preheat oven to 320°F.
2. In a large nonstick saucepan, mix the semolina with the coconut cream by adding coconut cream one cup at a time and stirring well while incorporating.
3. Add the caster sugar and continue stirring.
4. Bring to a boil over medium heat, stirring constantly.
5. When the mixture begins to thicken, add the butter and mix well.
6. Stop cooking when the dough pulls away from the sides of the pan. Add salt, ground cardamom and mix.
7. Separate the whites from the egg yolks.
8. Stir the yolks in the preparation, one by one, mixing well after adding each yolk.
9. Beat the egg whites until stiff and gently incorporate them into the preparation.
10. Pour into a baking pan lined with parchment paper and bake for 45 minutes in the preheated oven.
11. Sprinkle with sesame seeds right out of the oven.
12. Sanwin makin can be unmolded and eaten warm or cold. Cut into diamond shapes before serving.

21

Jack Fruit Sago Dessert

Country: Cambodia

Servings: 4

INGREDIENTS:
- ¼ C sago or tapioca pearls
- 2½ C coconut milk
- 1 pandan leaves (or 1 Tbs pandan extract)
- 1/3 C sugar
- ¼ Tsp salt
- 1 C jack fruit peeled, seeded, and cut into ½ inch strips
- 1 cup crushed ice or rice

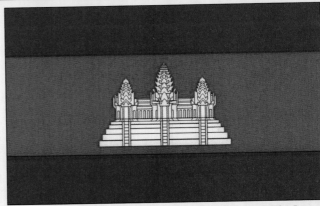

Tapioca pearls will work instead of sago! Find a sago recipe on page 188.

INSTRUCTIONS:

1. Cook sago (or tapioca pearls) in a pot of boiling water until translucent. Sago is cooked when center is no longer opaque, about 8 minutes. Pour sago into a sieve and rinse under running water to remove excessive starch. Drain well.

2. Combine coconut milk, pandan leaf, sugar, and salt in a medium size saucepan. Bring to a boil over medium low heat. Stir to dissolve sugar and salt.

3. Add jack fruit and cooked sago (or tapioca pearls). Bring it back up to a boil. Turn off stove.

4. Serve warm in small bowls with rice or, cold with crushed ice.

Country: Canada   **Servings: 4**

INGREDIENTS:
• 28 oz bag of frozen
seasoned fries
• 2 Tbs bacon fat
• 1 medium shallot, minced
• 1 garlic clove, minced
• 3 Tbs all-purpose flour
• 1½ C milk (you may
substitute chicken or beef
broth)
• ½ Tsp salt
• ½ Tsp pepper
• 1 Tbs Worcestershire sauce
• 1–2 C of Mozzarella cheese
• 2 C of cheddar cheese curds

Poutine was listed as one of Canada's top 10 inventions!

INSTRUCTIONS:
1. Bake fries according to package directions.
2. While the fries are baking, add 1/2 Tbs bacon fat in a medium skillet or sauce pan and heat over medium heat. Add shallots, stir and cook until soft. Reduce heat if necessary to avoid burning.
3. Add garlic to pan and stir, cooking for one additional minute.
4. Add flour and stir constantly. Continue cooking until the flour develops a golden color and starts to smell nutty.
5. While stirring continuously, slowly add liquid. Add salt, pepper and Worcestershire sauce and continue stirring until the gravy thickens to desired consistency. This may take 3-5 minutes and will come to a simmer. Keep stirring to avoid burning the bottom.
6. Plate out the hot fries, add the mozzarella and cheese curds, then pour hot gravy over. Serve immediately.

Country: Chile　　　　　　　　**Servings: 6**

INGREDIENTS:
• 2 ½ C of all-purpose flour
• 1 Tsp salt
• 1 C of warm/hot water, and more if needed
• 2 Tbs melted butter, still warm or shortening or lard
• 1 envelope quick yeast (1 Tbs)

This pairs perfectly with the Mahi Mahi on page 12

INSTRUCTIONS:
1. Make hole with the flour mixed with the salt and put melted butter in the center, add 1 cup of warm water and yeast, mix.
2. Knead until the dough is soft and pliable, takes about 10 minutes, add more water if you need..
3. Make a log with the dough and cut into 12 equal pieces, cover with a tea towel and work each ball into round discs.
4. Let rise for 1 1/2 hours in a warm place covered with a tea towel.
5. Preheat oven to 350°F
6. Pierce the rolls with a fork and paint with warm milk. Bake for 25 – 30 minutes or until lightly browned.
7. Serve hot, any extras reheat wrapped in a damp cloth in the microwave.

Chinese Pork and Shrimp Dumplings (Jiao Zi)

INGREDIENTS

For the dough:
• 6-3/4 oz. (1-1/2 cups) unbleached all-purpose flour; more for kneading

For the filling:
• 2 cups finely chopped napa cabbage
• Kosher salt
• 12 oz. ground pork
• 8 oz. peeled, deveined shrimp, coarsely chopped
• 3 medium scallions, thinly sliced
• 3 large cloves garlic, minced
• 2 Tbs. Shaoxing (Chinese rice wine) or dry sherry
• 1-1/2 Tbs. grated fresh ginger
• 1 Tbs. soy sauce
• 2 tsp. toasted Asian sesame oil
• 1/2 tsp. granulated sugar
• Freshly ground black pepper

The dough can be covered with plastic and refrigerated for up to 8 hours.

INSTRUCTIONS:

Make the dough:

1. Pour the flour into a mound on a clean work surface. Make a deep, wide well in the center and pour in 1/2 cup cold water. Stir with your fingers, staying in the center at first and being careful that the water doesn't breach the wall. Little by little, using your hand and a bench knife, mix in flour from the sides until the dough starts to come together.
(Alternatively, put the flour in a medium bowl. Make a well, add the water, and stir first with a spoon and then your hand.)

2. If the dough remains in shreds, sprinkle in additional water, a teaspoon at a time, until it begins to stick together. Don't add too much water or the dough will be difficult to work.

3. Knead the dough for 5 minutes to form a smooth, firm, elastic ball.
(If you began the dough in a bowl, lightly dust a clean, dry surface with flour before kneading.) The dough should not be sticky and should bounce back when pressed with a fingertip.

4. Divide in half with a bench knife and roll into two 6-inch logs. Sprinkle each log evenly with flour, cover with a clean kitchen towel, and let rest for at least 30 minutes at room temperature before rolling and filling.

Make the filling:

In a medium bowl, toss the cabbage with 2 tsp. salt and set aside for 30 minutes to shed moisture. Wring out in a clean kitchen towel to extract as much liquid as possible.

In a large bowl, combine the cabbage with the pork, shrimp, scallions, garlic, Shaoxing, ginger, soy sauce, sesame oil, sugar, and 1/4 tsp. pepper.

Stir until well mixed. Refrigerate for at least 20 minutes.

Cut and roll the dough:

1. Cut each log in half crosswise. Cut each half crosswise into thirds, and then slice each of those pieces into three even coins. You should have 36 pieces of equal size. Toss the pieces in flour to coat evenly and then cover with a clean towel so they don't dry out.

2. Using a small rolling pin, roll a piece of dough into a thin 3-inch circle; with the dough in one hand and the pin in the other, roll from the edges toward the center as you rotate the dough.

Fill and shape the dumplings:

1. Spoon 1 to 2 tsp. of the filling onto a dough circle, fold it in half, and then if you're going to boil the dumplings, seal it by pinching along the curved edge.

If you're planning to pan-fry the dumplings for pot stickers, make your first pinch at the center of the curved edge and then pleat toward the center on both sides to create a rounded belly. This wider shape allows the dumplings to sit upright in the pan and form a flat surface for browning.

2. Repeat with the remaining wrappers and filling.

To cook:

1. Bring a large (7- to 8-quart) pot of salted water to a boil. Working in 2 or 3 batches to avoid overcrowding, quickly add the dumplings one at a time, making sure they don't stick to each other.

2. Lower the heat to medium and continue to boil, gently stirring occasionally, until the dumplings float and are cooked through, 3 to 5 minutes. Remove with a slotted spoon and serve immediately with your choice of dipping sauce.

Pan-fry:

1. Heat 2 Tbs. vegetable oil in a heavy-duty 10- or 12-inch skillet over medium-high heat until shimmering. Working quickly and in batches if necessary (adding more oil for the second batch if needed), arrange the dumplings belly side down in concentric circles starting from the outer edge.

2. Cook until golden brown on the bottom, 1 to 2 minutes. Pour in about 1/2 cup water or enough to come about a third of the way up the sides of the dumplings, bring to a boil, cover, and cook until all of the water has been absorbed, 2 to 3 minutes.

3. Remove the lid, reduce the heat to medium, and continue cooking just until the dumplings are dry and crisp on the bottom, 1 to 2 minutes.

4. Loosen the dumplings from the pan with a spatula. Invert the pan over a plate to flip the dumplings, browned side up, onto the plate (or transfer with a spatula). Serve immediately with your choice of dipping sauce.

Country: Columbia

Servings: 9

INGREDIENTS:
- 1 pkg. Pepperidge Farm Puff Pastry Sheets
- 1 bar guava paste
- 1 pkg. Cream cheese

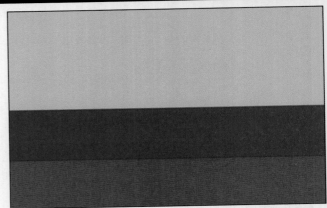

Make sure to grab puff pastry, not phyllo dough!

INSTRUCTIONS:

1. Preheat oven to 400°F

2. Thaw the puff pastry according to package directions.

3. Use baking parchment to line your cookie sheet so the guava won't stick.

4. Unfold one of the pastry sheets and place on pan.

5. Cut guava into 1/4 inch slices and place on the pastry sheet.

6. Spread cream cheese over guava paste slices

7. Unfold second pastry sheet and place on top of guava paste.

8. Cut to desired size before baking.

9. Bake at 400°F for 25 to 35 minutes or until golden brown.

Picadillo de Chayote

INGREDIENTS:
- 1lb minced beef
- 4 pcs Chayote, peeled, seeded and cubed
- 1 C corn kernels
- 1 can chopped tomatoes
- 1½ Tbs sugar
- 4 cloves garlic, minced
- 1 white onion, chopped
- 1 Tsp dried sweet basil
- 1 Tsp dried oregano
- salt
- freshly ground black pepper
- olive oil

Can't find chayote? Use potatoes!

INSTRUCTIONS:

1. In a pot, sauté onion, garlic and tomatoes in olive oil.

2. Add minced beef and cook until it turns light brown.

3. Add chayote and cook for 3 minutes

4. Add corn kernels, chopped tomatoes, sugar, dried sweet basil and dried oregano then bring to a boil then simmer for 10-15 minutes or until chayote is tender

5. Season with freshly ground black pepper and salt.

Country: Croatia   **Servings: 4**

INGREDIENTS: (Equal Parts)
• Olive oil
• Feta cheese
• Tomatoes
• Green onions
• Pita bread
• Greek seasoning

There's no measurements because it's up to you how much you want to make! Use equal amounts, and add olive oil to taste.

INSTRUCTIONS:

1. Dice your tomatoes and green onions.
2. Then pour the olive oil onto a large plate.
3. Now add the diced vegetables.
4. Then cover with a generous amount of feta cheese.
5. Now sprinkle your Greek seasoning over the entire dish.
6. Finally, take a spoon and stir the
ingredients together, ensuring that everything is coated with olive oil.
7. Serve in a bowl with big chunks of pita bread.

Crock Pot Mojo Pork

Country: Cuba   **Servings: 4**

INGREDIENTS:
- 1 bone-in pork shoulder (about 4lbs) pork butt works as well)
- 1½ Tsp salt
- 1 Tsp ground black pepper
- ¾ C orange juice, freshly squeezed
- ½ C lime juice, freshly squeezed
- Zest of 1 orange
- Zest of 1 lime
- ½ C olive oil
- 8 cloves garlic, chopped finely
- 2 Tsp dried oregano
- 2 Tsp ground cumin
- ¼ C chopped cilantro (lightly packed)

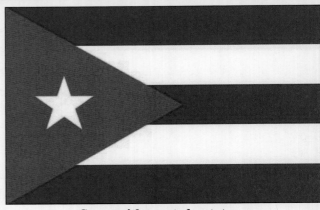

Serve with roasted potatoes and bread, or on a cubano!

INSTRUCTIONS:
1. Using a paring knife, make a few slits all over the surface of the pork.
2. To the slow cooker, add the rest of the ingredients. Mix to combine.
3. Place the pork in the slow cooker and cook on high for 5 - 6 hours or on low for 8 - 10 hours. 4. The pork should be tender and almost falling of the bone!. Carefully remove it from the slow cooker and place it onto an aluminum foil lined baking sheet.
5. Bake at 400°F for about 15 to 20 minutes or until browned.
6. Remove from the oven and let it rest for 10 minutes before serving. You will be able to shred the meat with a couple of forks.
7. Serve with the remaining juices from the slow cooker.

Country: Denmark   **Servings: 4**

INGREDIENTS:
- 3 lbs potatoes
- 1 large white onion
- 1 bay leaf
- 1 lb curly kale
- 1 Tsp salt
- 1 pinch ground pepper
- 1 lb smoked sausage
- ½ C milk
- 2 Tbs butter

Great as a side, or a main dish!

INSTRUCTIONS:
1. Peel and dice potatoes and onion.

2. Clean, trim and slice kale.

3. Add the potatoes, onion, kale, a bay leaf, a pinch of salt in a pot, with just enough water to cover all.

4. Cover and boil gently for about 25 minutes.

5. Meanwhile steam or grill the smoked sausage until done then slice into bite size pieces.

6. Remove the bay leaf, drain the vegetables, and mash them.

7. Add milk and butter.

8. Add in sliced smoked sausage.

9. Add salt and pepper to taste and serve.

Dulce De Platano Maduro (Caramelized Sweet Plantains)

Country: Dominican Republic   Servings: 4

INGREDIENTS:
- 2 Sweet Plantains
- 1 Tsp of Sugar (for oil)
- ¼ C of cooking oil
- ½ C of brown sugar
- 2 Cinnamon Sticks
- 1 Tbs of Sugar (For plantains)
- 3 Cloves

Make sure you get sweet plantains, not green!

INSTRUCTIONS:
1. Cut sweet plantains into 3-inch pieces
2. Set stove to medium-high heat. In a pan, add the cooking oil. Once the oil is hot, add 1 teaspoon of sugar. Wait until the sugar turns golden brown.
3. Add sweet plantain pieces to the pan and flip continuously until golden brown.
4. Reduce the heat to medium-heat. Add ¼ cup of water, 1 tablespoon of sugar, brown sugar, cinnamon sticks and cloves. Sir all ingredients together.
5. Add 2 tablespoons of water and cover pan for about 10- 15 minutes.
6. Serve warm with vanilla ice cream

42

Fried Cheese Empanadas

Country: Ecuador   **Servings: 6**

INGREDIENTS:

For the Dough:
- 3 C all-purpose flour
- 1 Tsp salt
- ½ Tsp baking powder
- 8 Tbs cold butter
- ½ C cold milk or water

For the Filling:
- ¼ C minced white onion
- 1 Tbs butter
- 1 ½ C Monterey Jack cheese (shredded; or other cheese such as cheddar, Gouda, etc.)
- 1 quart vegetable oil (for frying; or as needed)
- ¼ C sugar

Use this dough for a ton of other recipes (like the piroskis on page 132!)

INSTRUCTIONS:

1. Place the flour in a large bowl with the salt and baking powder and whisk briefly to mix.

2. Cut the butter into small pieces and add it to the flour. Use a pastry cutter or 2 knives to "cut" the butter into the flour, until the mixture is crumbly and there are no large pieces of butter.

3. Add the milk or water 2 tablespoons at a time and mix gently with a fork. Continue to mix until the dough comes together and is not too dry or shaggy (you made need slightly more or less water).

4. Knead the dough a few times with your hands until it is relatively smooth 5.Wrap it tightly in plastic wrap and let it rest on the counter for 30 minutes 6.Cover dough with plastic wrap and set aside for 30 minutes

FILLING:

1. Melt the butter in a small skillet and add the minced onion. Cook over medium-low heat until the onion is translucent and fragrant.

2. Remove from heat and let cool.

3. When it has cooled, place the onion with the shredded cheese in a bowl and toss to combine.

SHAPING/COOKING:

1. Divide the dough into 16 equal balls. Roll each piece of dough into a ball, and then let the dough rest for 5 minutes.

2. On a lightly floured surface, roll each ball of dough into a thin,6-inch diameter circle, letting the dough rest for several minutes if needed to let the dough relax and stretch.

3. Brush the edges of a circle of dough lightly with water.

4. Place 1 ½ tablespoons of the cheese mixture in the middle of the dough, and then fold the circle of dough in half and seal the edges together firmly. 5. Fold the edges of the dough into a decorative seam (learn how to shape and fill Empanadas).

6. Repeat with remaining pieces of dough.

7. Heat several inches of vegetable oil in a deep skillet or saucepan over medium-high heat.

8. The oil is hot enough with a piece of the dough sizzles gently in the oil. 9. Cook the Empanadas in batches, flipping them once until they are golden brown.

10. Carefully remove the Empanadas from the oil with a slotted spoon, spatula, or tongs, and place them on a plate lined with paper towels.

11. Sprinkle the tops of the Empanadas with a teaspoon of sugar as soon as you place them on the plate.

12. Let Empanadas cool for 5 minutes before serving.

Country: Egypt   **Servings: 3 dozen cookies**

INGREDIENTS:
• 4 C flour
• 2 ½ sticks unsalted butter
• ½ C powdered sugar
• ¾ Tsp baking powder
• 1 pinch salt
• ¼ Tsp vanilla extract
• ¼ Tsp cinnamon
• ¼ Tsp nutmeg
• ½ C milk

This dough is perfect to make and freeze for later.

INSTRUCTIONS:
1. Preheat oven to 350°F and line 2-3 baking sheets with parchment paper.
2. In a large bowl or mixer, mix together all the dry ingredients: flour, sugar, baking powder, salt, cinnamon and nutmeg.
3. With mixer set to low speed, slowly add vanilla followed by melted butter and continue mixing - pausing just before the dough fully forms.
4. Pour in milk and mix until all ingredients are fully incorporated.
5. Scoop a rounded tablespoonful of dough and roll into a ball. Place on a cookie sheets. Make a cross hatch on the top using a fork, pressing down slightly.
6. Bake each batch for 12-15 minutes, or until bottom edges are slightly browned. Cool completely before dusting generously with powdered sugar.

Country: El Salvador   **Servings: 6**

INGREDIENTS:
• 2 C Maseca Instant Corn
Masa Mix (not the kind for
Tamales)
• 1½ C water
• 2 Tbs vegetable oil
• ¼ Tsp salt
• 1 C re-fried beans
• 1 C shredded mozzarella
cheese (or quesillo if you can
find it)
• additional water and oil for
your hands

Find the flour on Amazon!

INSTRUCTIONS:
1. Mix maseca, water, oil, and salt in a medium bowl until well combined.
Dough should be moist and have the texture of play-dough. It should not crack
when pinched. If dough is too dry, add more water, 1 tablespoon at a time until
the right consistency is reached.
2. Cover dough and allow it to rest while mixing the filling.
3. Heat re-fried beans for 30 seconds in the microwave to soften. Combine
with shredded cheese.
4. Divide dough into 10 equally sized portions and form into balls.
5. Wet hands with a bit of water and vegetable oil to prevent sticking.
6. Press dough ball out flat until its about 1/2″ thick.
7. Add 2 tablespoons of filling mixture into the center of the dough.
8. Pinch the dough closed around the filling until it forms a ball again.
9. Gently press the ball back out flat until it's about 1/2″ thick again.
10. Place onto a lightly-oiled griddle over medium heat for about 2 minutes per
side, or until pupusa surface begins to brown and blister.
11. Serve hot with salsa.

Country: Ethiopia   **Servings: 8**

INGREDIENTS:
• ½ C olive or canola oil
• 2 C carrots sliced about 4
medium carrots
• 1 medium onion chopped
• 2-3 Tsp minced garlic
• 1 Tbs curry powder or turmeric
• 1- Tsp cumin
• 1½ Tsp smoked paprika
• 1 large tomato diced
• 1 lbs potatoes cut in chunks
• 1 bell pepper chopped
• 8 C chopped cabbage about ½
cabbage head
• ½ Tsp cayenne pepper or more to
taste optional
• salt and pepper to taste

A great vegetarian meal that you can easily add protein to!

INSTRUCTIONS:
1.In a large saucepan or Dutch oven, heat oil over medium heat.

2. Add onions, give it a minute or two then add, carrots, potatoes and tomatoes.

3. Stir in all the spices; garlic, cumin, smoked paprika, curry, white pepper, cayenne pepper, and salt.

4. Simmer for about 5 minutes, stirring occasionally to prevent burns.

5. Pour in about 1 cup water to the saucepan , you may have to add more if needed. Continue to simmer for about 10-15 minutes until the potatoes is almost tender.

6. Finally add cabbage and green pepper, stir Continue cooking for about 5 minutes.

7. Adjust for seasonings. Serve warm

Fijian Banana Cake

INGREDIENTS:
- 2 C sugar
- 4 Tbs butter
- 4 eggs
- 5 C of self raising flour (or plain flour with 5 Tsp of baking powder)
- 1½ C of milk or coconut milk
- 4 bananas

This cake goes perfect with milk or tea!
Like teh tarik on page 96.

INSTRUCTIONS:
1. Pre-heat the oven to 350°F
2. Beat the sugar and butter together until soft
3. Beat in the eggs (one at a time) until the sugar is dissolved and the mixture is fluffy
4. Add the flour (little by little) to make a very soft dough
5. Mash the bananas and stir these into the mixture
6. Add the milk and mix all together
7. Grease the cake tray and then pour in the mixture
8. Bake for 45 minutes

Easy Icing:
1. Mix together 7 tablespoons of Icing Sugar and 3 tablespoons butter
2. When the cake is baked and smelling delicious, leave to cool
3. Then spread the icing sugar thickly (very important) all over the cake

Lohikeitto (Finnish Salmon Soup)

Country: Finland　　　　　　　　**Servings: 6**

INGREDIENTS:
• ½ stick (¼ C) unsalted
butter
• 1 leek, sliced (white and
light green parts only)
• 5 C fish stock (can be
substituted with water)
• 1 lb potatoes, cubed
• 1 carrot, sliced
• 1 lb salmon fillet, de-boned,
de-skinned and cut into small
chunks
• 1 C heavy cream
• 1 C fresh dill for garnish,
finely chopped
• salt and pepper to taste

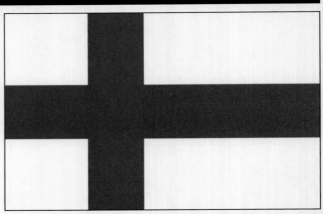

**If you don't have fish stock, veggie stock
also works!**

INSTRUCTIONS:
1. Melt the butter in a pot. Add the sliced leek and saute until translucent,
about 7 minutes.
2. Add the stock, carrot and potatoes. Bring to a boil and cook for about 10
minutes over medium heat. At this point the potatoes should be almost ready.
3. Add the salmon chunks and the cream, and cook for about 5-7 minutes
more, until it starts to boil.
4. Turn off the heat and add the dill, salt and pepper. Close the lid and wait for
another 10 minutes.
5. Serve with crusty bread.

Crockpot Coq A Vin

Country: France   **Servings: 4**

INGREDIENTS:
• 2-3 slices thick cut bacon, chopped
• 1 yellow onion, chopped
• 4 cloves garlic, minced or grated
• 2 Tb tomato paste
• 4 carrots, chopped
• 1½ lbs boneless chicken breasts
• 2 C cremini mushrooms, sliced
• 1½ C dry red wine, such as Cabernet, or red cooking wine
• 1 C low sodium chicken broth
• 2 bay leaves
• 4 thyme sprigs
• kosher salt and black pepper
• 1½ C fresh parsley, chopped

Leave the lid off the Crockpot during the last hour to let all the alcohol evaporate.

INSTRUCTIONS:
1. Cook the bacon in a large skillet over medium heat until crisp, about 5 minutes. If there's excess bacon grease, drain off all but 1 tablespoon.
2. To the skillet, add the onion, garlic, and tomato paste and cook an additional 5 minutes.
Remove from the heat and transfer the mixture to the bowl of your slow cooker.
3. To the slow cooker, add in the red wine, chicken broth, bay leaves, thyme, chicken, carrots, and mushrooms. Season with salt and pepper. Cover and cook on low for 6-7 hours or on high for 4-5 hours.
4. Once done cooking, cook, uncovered on high for 15-20 minutes to reduce the sauce. Remove the bay leaves and thyme and discard. Stir in the parsley and reserved bacon.
5. Serve the chicken and sauce over vegetables.

Country: Germany   **Servings:4**

INGREDIENTS:
FOR THE SPÄTZLE:
- 2 ½ C flour
- ½ teaspoon salt
- 1/3 cup water
- 1/3 cup milk
- 3 eggs
- Butter for finishing

FOR THE SAUCE:
- 5 tablespoons butter divided
- 1 shallot finely chopped
- 1½ pounds mushrooms sliced
- 1 ounce white wine
- 1 Tbs tomato paste
- 2 C broth
- ½ C cream
- Bunch of flat leaf parsley chopped

**Use a second slotted spoon to drop in the Spätzle
if you don't have a grater.**

INSTRUCTIONS:
TO MAKE THE SPÄTZLE:
1. In a large bowl mix together the flour and salt. Add the water, milk and eggs to a measuring cup and whisk together well.
2. Pour into the bowl with the flour and immediately start vigorously stirring the batter with a wooden spoon until there are no more lumps and you start seeing bubbles forming. Cover and rest for 30 minutes.
3. When ready to make the Spätzle bring a large pot of salted water to the boil. Heat a large frying pan over medium heat and add a knob of butter to it.
4. Place a coarse metal grater (or a special Spätzle maker if you own one) over the pot. Add about 1/3 cup of batter on top of the grater and gently stroke over it with the back of a spoon. Remove the grater and let the Spätzle cook until they come to the surface. Remove with a slotted spoon and drop into the hot pan. Proceed the same way with the remaining batter, adding more butter to the pan as needed.

TO MAKE THE SAUCE:
1. Heat a large frying pan over medium high heat and add three tablespoons of butter to it. Add the shallot to the pan and cook until starting to brown.
2. Add the mushrooms and continue to cook until softened. De glaze with the white wine and cook until reduced. Add the broth and tomato paste, reduce to a simmer and cook until reduced to a thick sauce. Finish with the remaining two tablespoons of butter and the cream.
3. Serve on top of the Spätzle and garnish with chopped parsley.

Country: Greece   **Servings: 6**

INGREDIENTS:
For the Tzatziki Sauce:
- 1 medium cucumber
- 1 C plain Greek yogurt
- 1 Tbs extra virgin olive oil
- 1 Tbs lemon juice
- 2 Tbs. chopped fresh dill
- 1 medium clove garlic
pressed or minced
- ¼ Tsp salt

For the Gyro:
- Pita bread
- Shredded iceberg lettuce
- Sliced tomatoes
- Sliced cucumbers
- Sliced onion
- Feta cheese

Find the recipes for the meats on page 184.

INSTRUCTIONS:
1. Prepare the meat for the gyros
(found on page 35)
2. Make the tzatziki. Grate the cucumber and squeeze the excess liquid out with your hands. Discard the liquid. Place the cucumber in a mixing bowl with the rest of the tzatziki ingredients and mix well.
3.Cook the meat. Heat a large, non-stick skillet over medium-high heat. Add the chicken/lamb slices and cook for about 4-5 minutes on each side, until cooked through.
4.Make the Gyro. Warm the pita bread (in the oven or microwave). Add a bit of shredded lettuce, tomato, cucumber, onion, and chicken on top. Drizzle with a generous amount of tzatziki and feta cheese, if desired. Fold the gyro in half and serve.

Country: Guatemala   **Servings: 4**

INGREDIENTS:

• 2 Tbs Corn Oil, divided
• 3 lbs. bone-in, skin-on chicken pieces (like breasts, thighs and/or legs)
• Adobo All-Purpose Seasoning with Pepper, to taste
• ¼ medium onion, finely chopped (about ½ C)
• ½ green bell pepper, finely chopped (about ½ C)
• ½ red bell pepper, finely chopped (about ½ C)
• 1 packet Sazón GOYA® with Coriander and Annatto
• 1 can (25.5 oz.) Coconut Milk
• ¼ C finely chopped fresh cilantro

This dish is great over rice or in a taco.

INSTRUCTIONS:

1. Heat 1 tbsp. oil in large, deep skillet over medium-high heat. Using paper towels, pat chicken dry; season all over with Adobo. Add chicken pieces to skillet skin-side down. Cook, flipping once, until golden brown on both sides, about 10 minutes. Transfer chicken to plate.

2. Pour remaining oil into skillet. Stir in onions and bell peppers. Cook, stirring occasionally, until vegetables are soft, about 7 minutes. Sprinkle Sazón over vegetables; cook until fragrant, about 30 seconds more.

3. Pour coconut milk into skillet with vegetables. Transfer chicken to skillet skin-side up, arranging in single layer; bring coconut milk to boil. Reduce heat to medium-low. Simmer, cover, then baste chicken occasionally with sauce, until chicken is cooked through (internal temperature will register 165°F), about 25 minutes.

4. Transfer chicken to platter; loosely cover with foil. Increase heat to medium-high. Simmer coconut milk sauce, stirring occasionally, until sauce thickens slightly. Stir in cilantro; season with Adobo, if desired.

5. To serve, pour sauce over chicken. Serve with rice and tortillas.

Yuca Cake

INGREDIENTS:

- 4 C Yuca Mashed
- 2 C Sugar
- 2 ½ C Coconut Milk
- 1/4 C Coconut Oil
- 1½ Tsp Cinnamon
- 2 Tbs Vanilla
- 2 Tsp Salt

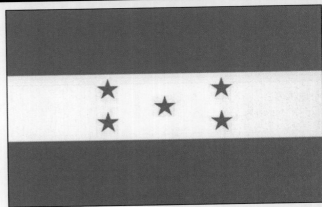

Check your frozen section for grated cassava root to save your arms some trouble!

INSTRUCTIONS:

1. Peel and chop Yuca.
2. Preheat oven to 350˚ Fahrenheit
3. Blend Yuca in a food processor.
4. Add sugar, coconut milk, coconut oil, cinnamon, vanilla, and salt.
5. Pour into a greased pan.
6. Bake for 1.5 to 2 hours. Insert a knife in the middle for doneness, if it comes out clean, it's ready!

Chicken Paprikash

INGREDIENTS:
- 3 eggs, beaten
- ½ C water
- 2½ C all-purpose flour
- 2 Tsp salt
- ¼ C butter
- 1½ lbs bone-in chicken pieces, with skin
- 1 medium onion, chopped
- 1½ cups water
- 1 Tb paprika
- ½ Tsp salt
- 1 Tsp ground black pepper
- 2 Tbs all-purpose flour
- 1 C sour cream

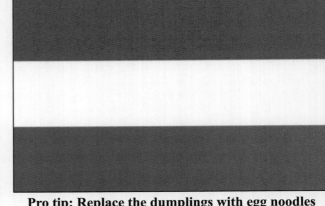

Pro tip: Replace the dumplings with egg noodles or rice if you're short on time.

INSTRUCTIONS:
1. Fill a large pot with water and bring to a boil over high heat. In a large bowl, mix together the eggs, 2 teaspoons of salt, and 1/2 cup of water. Gradually stir in 2 1/2 cups of flour to make a stiff batter. Using two spoons, scoop out some batter with one spoon and use the second to scrap off the spoonful of batter into the boiling water. Repeat until several dumplings are cooking. Cook dumplings for 10 minutes or until they float to the top; then lift from the water and drain in a colander or sieve. Rinse with warm water.
2. In a large skillet over medium-high heat, melt butter and add chicken; cook until lightly browned, turning once. Add onion to skillet and cook 5 to 8 minutes more. Pour in 1 1/2 cups of water, and season with paprika, salt, and pepper; cook 10 minutes more, or until chicken is cooked through and juices run clear. Remove chicken from skillet and keep warm.
3. Stir 2 tablespoons of flour into sour cream; then slowly stir into the onion mixture remaining in the skillet. Bring the mixture to a boil, stirring constantly, and cook until thickened.
4. To serve, add dumplings to the sour cream/onion mixture.

Brúnaðar Kartöflur (Icelandic Caramelized Potatoes)

Country: Iceland   **Servings: 4**

INGREDIENTS:
- 2 lbs. small potatoes
- ⅓ C sugar
- 2 Tbs water
- 3 Tbs unsalted butter

Small potatoes like red or fingerling potatoes work best.

INSTRUCTIONS:
1. Boil the potatoes in large pot of water until tender.
2. Drain potatoes and let cool until you can peel them.
3. Peel them and set aside
4. In a saucepan, add sugar and water to pan and simmer over medium heat until syrup turns a golden brown.
5. stir in the butter and then the potatoes
6. Cook to combine all the ingredients, about 5 more minutes, taking care that all the potatoes are covered with the caramel.

Country: India   **Servings: 6**

INGREDIENTS:
- 2 Tbs coconut oil
- 2 Tbs curry powder
- 1 Tsp paprika
- 1 Tsp cumin
- 1 Tsp turmeric powder
- 2 sprigs fresh thyme, or 1 Tsp dried
- 1 C onion, finely chopped
- 4 cloves garlic, mince
- 1 Tsp fresh ginger, grated
- 2 green onions, chopped
- 20 ounce can green jack fruit, drained and rinsed
- 4 medium potatoes, cubed
- 1 medium carrot, diced
- 15 ounce can coconut milk
- 2 C vegetable broth, or 2 cubes vegetable bouillon plus water
- 1 Tsp Italian seasoning

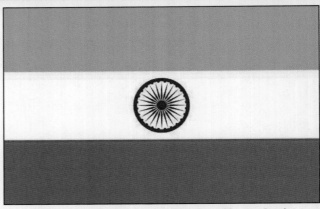

Replace jack fruit with chicken if you don't want a vegetarian dish.

INSTRUCTIONS:
1. Plug in your Instant Pot and press saute mode button. Add oil, once heated add dry spices, curry powder, paprika, cumin, turmeric, thyme and cook for a minute stirring constantly.

2. Add onion, garlic, ginger, spring onion and cook until for 2 minutes or until onions are soft. Add jack fruit, potato, carrots and stir to coat.

3. Add coconut milk, vegetable broth or bouillon plus water, Italian seasoning, cayenne pepper, and stir. 4. Close Instant Pot lid and press manual mode for 10 minutes. When finished, allow Instant Pot to natural release for 10 minutes. Carefully release the knob to release the remaining pressure. Remove lid, stir in cilantro leaves, crush some of the potatoes to thicken curry and check seasonings.

Country: Indonesia   **Servings: 4**

INGREDIENTS
Skin:
• 2¼ C flour
• 4 eggs
• dash of salt
• 1½ C thin coconut milk (add up to 1 C if not watery enough)
• ½ Tsp pandan extract (adjust to the desired color)
• Margarine

Filling:
• ½ C coconut (grated)
• ¾ C of brown sugar
• ½ C water
• 2 pandan leaves (or 1 Tb extract)
• Butter

Find Pandan extract online on Amazon!

INSTRUCTIONS:

Filling:
1. Mix all filling ingredients until the contents become one
2. Add water, then heat over a low heat.
3. Stir until evenly heated.

Skin:
1. Mix flour, eggs and salt in a bowl.
2. Add milk little by little, then stir until smooth
3. Add the pandan extract to the dough for coloring.
4. Preheat the frying pan and make thin omelet, then dab with margarine
5. Fill all omelet with coconut dough, roll the dough / fold

Country: Iran   **Servings: 6**

INGREDIENTS:
- 2 C basmati rice white
- 3 Tbs olive oil
- 1 onion medium, chopped
- 3 cloves garlic grated
- 1 lb lamb, ground, 90% lean
- 1 Tsp curry powder
- 1 Tsp cayenne pepper
- ½ Tsp cumin ground
- 1 Tsp turmeric
- ½ Tsp black pepper
- 1 Tsp thyme or savory, dried
- 1¼ Tsp salt adjust as needed
- 1 Tsp lemon powder dried or 2 tablespoons lemon juice
- 1 lb green beans cut into 1/2 inch or frozen
- 6 ounces tomato paste
- 1/3 Tsp saffron powdered and dissolved in 2 tablespoons hot water

No saffron? Just add a little extra curry!

INSTRUCTIONS:
Cook Ground Meat with Green Beans
1. Heat 2 tablespoons olive oil at medium setting in a cooking pot. Add the chopped onions and sauté few minutes. Then add the grated garlic and continue to sauté until the onions are light golden brown.
2. Add the ground lamb and sauté. Then add all the spices, dried herbs, 1/2 tsp salt (/curry powder through lemon powder) and stir for 2 to 3 minutes. Add the green beans.
3. Next add the tomato paste and mix it well. If the mixture is too thick, may add a some water, cover and let it simmer until the beans are 3/4th done. It will continue to cook in the steaming process in the next steps. The mixture should be moist but not too wet.
Cook Rice
1. Rinse the white basmati rice in water several times until the water is clear and not starchy. Then drain the rice very well in a colander
2. Bring 6 cups of water and 1 tablespoon salt to a boil. Add the rice and allow it to boil at medium high heat for about 5 to 6 minutes until the rice grains are soft. Stir the rice in between. Drain the rice and set aside.
Assemble Rice with Meat/Green Beans
1. Place the cooked rice with the sautéed meat/green bean mixture in several alternating layers in a heavy bottomed wide cooking pot. Sprinkle 1 tablespoon olive oil and saffron water all over.

Country: Ireland   **Servings: 6**

INGREDIENTS:
• 2 1/2 lbs Yukon Gold potatoes, peeled and sliced 1/2" thick
• Fresh ground black pepper
• 12 ounces thick-cut bacon (see notes)
• 6 bratwurst sausages, or bangers if you can find them
• 2 large white onions, peeled and sliced into 1/2" rings
• 1 14-ounce can chicken broth (low-sodium preferred)
• 2 Tbs apple cider vinegar
• 1 C beer (plus more if needed)
• ¼ C minced fresh parsley, divided

Don't have a dutch oven? Cook in a crock pot instead! Change the time to 6 hours on low, follow original directions.

INSTRUCTIONS:
1. Preheat oven to 300°F
2. Lightly oil a 12-inch Camp Dutch Oven and the inside of the lid.
3. Layer the sliced potatoes in a shingle pattern on the bottom of the Dutch Oven. Sprinkle the potatoes with about 2 teaspoons fresh ground pepper.
4. Cook the bacon in a skillet until crisp. Drain on a paper towel lined plate and set aside. Once cooled crumble the bacon. Lightly brown the sausages in the bacon fat but do not fully cook. Set aside.
5. Remove all but about 3 tablespoons of the bacon fat and discard. Add the sliced onions to the hot skillet and cook covered for 5-7 minutes stirring once or twice. Remove the lid and add the chicken broth, vinegar and season with black pepper. Bring the onions and broth to a boil. Remove from the heat and carefully pour the onions and broth over the potatoes in the dutch oven.
6. Top the onions and potatoes with half the crumbled bacon and half the chopped parsley. Place the browned sausages on top and cover with the lid.
7. Cook the coddle for about an hour. Check the casserole to make sure it does not dry out and burn. After an hour add 1 cup or more of your favorite beer to the pot. Continue cooking until the sausages are fully cooked and golden brown - about 2-3 hours.
8.Garnish with the remaining parsley and bacon.

Country: Israel　　　　　　　　　**Servings: 6**

INGREDIENTS:
Vegetable Saute:
- 2 Tbs olive oil
- 1 C yellow onion, sliced
- 2 cloves garlic, minced
- 1½ C baby portobello mushrooms
- 6 C spinach
- ½ Tsp sea salt
- ½ Tsp black pepper
- ¼ C vegetable broth

Couscous:
- 1 Tbs olive oil
- 1 C Israeli couscous
- 2 C water

Toast the Couscous for a deeper flavor.

INSTRUCTIONS:
Spinach and Mushrooms

1. In a large pot, bring 2 tablespoons of oil to medium heat. Add onion and sauté for 3-5 minutes, until they are softened and translucent. Add garlic and sauté for 2 minutes.

2. Add mushrooms and sauté for 5 minutes.

3. Add spinach, salt and pepper, and broth and stir to combine. Cover and cook until spinach is wilted. About 5 minutes.

4. Remove from heat and set aside.

Couscous

1. In a medium pot, bring 2 tablespoons of oil to medium heat. Pour in the couscous and stir to coat with oil. Cook for 2 minutes, until the couscous starts to smell toasted.

2. Pour in 2 cups of water and bring to a boil.

3. Once boiling, decrease the heat to a simmer and cover. Cook for 10 minutes, or until al dente, stirring occasionally. Drain off excess liquid.

4. Combine couscous with spinach and mushroom mixture and stir to combine.

Tiramisu

INGREDIENTS:
- 1 C heavy whipping cream
- 1 C mascarpone cheese, room temperature
- 1/3 C sugar
- 1 Tsp vanilla extract
- 1 Tbs Amaretto liquor or Brandy (optional)
- 2 C espresso or STRONG coffee at room temperature
- 1 pack Ladyfingers (Boudoir biscuits/ Savoiardi.)
- Cocoa powder for dusting the top

Lady Fingers can be found in the cookie section of most stores.

INSTRUCTIONS:
1. Beat whipping cream, sugar, and vanilla until soft peaks form.
2. Add in mascarpone cheese and amaretto (if using) and continue to whip to stiff peaks.
3. Dip ladyfingers in coffee (and brandy if using) and place in an 8×8 pan to make the first layer – you can fit about 7 cookies in each layer. Don't let them soak as the will fall apart, just a quick dunk in the coffee is enough.
4. Spread half of the whipped cream mixture on top of the first layer of ladyfingers. Repeat process with the second layer of ladyfingers and cream mixture.
5. Dust the top of dessert with cocoa powder using a sieve. Refrigerate for about 2-4 hours.

Jamaican Oxtail

INGREDIENTS:
- 2.5-3.5 lbs beef oxtail
- ¼ C low-sodium soy sauce
- 3 Tbs vegetable or canola oil
- 2 Tbs ground Jamaican allspice
- 1 Tbs minced garlic
- 1 Tbs brown sugar
- 1 Tsp ground ginger or grated fresh ginger
- 1 lime, juiced
- 1 C diced sweet onions
- 4 C water
- 1 habanero pepper
- Fresh thyme sprigs
- Green onions, for garnishing (optional)

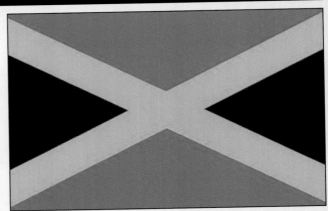

Don't have a pressure cooking? Cook in a Crockpot on high for 6 hours instead!

INSTRUCTIONS:
1. Mix marinade ingredients: soy sauce, 2 tbsp vegetable oil, allspice, garlic, brown sugar, ginger, lime juice, and thyme sprigs.
2. Place oxtail in gallon size resealable bag or large bowl. Pour marinade over oxtails and mix to cover evenly.
3. Marinate for at least 6 hours.
4. Heat 1 tbsp oil in large pressure cooker.
5. Sear oxtail on all sides in batches, set aside on clean plate.
6. Carefully pour out all but about 1 tsp of the oil/ rendered fat out the pan. Be very careful with the hot oil.
7. Saute onions until translucent.
8. Add browned oxtails and water.
9. Cover and bring to pressure according to manufacturer's instructions.
10. Once at pressure, cook 60 minutes.
11. Remove from heat and let pressure pot cool naturally until safe to open.
12. Taste and add additional seasoning as desired.
13. To thicken broth, cook pot uncovered over medium-high heat until the liquid reduces about 50%

Country: Japan   **Servings: 8**

INGREDIENTS:
• 4 egg whites
• 2 C flour
• 1 3/4 C water
• shrimp and/or veggies
• 1 tsp salt
• 1 tsp garlic powder

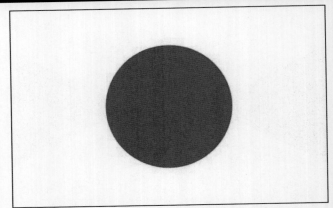

Use shrimp, squid, and veggies in your batter!

INSTRUCTIONS:
1. Mix egg whites, flour and water, keeping your rinsed and prepared shrimp and/or veggies to the side.
2. Heat a pan of oil until it is hot enough to bubble when a small drop of batter is put in.
3. When batter is smooth use a fork to dip your shrimp or veggies into the mix and place in hot oil to fry to perfection.
4. Place on paper towel when out of oil and nicely browned to absorb the excess oil.

Larb

INGREDIENTS:

For the Toasted Rice Powder
- 1 Tbs uncooked jasmine rice

For the pork:
- 1 lb ground pork or chicken
- fresh juice from ½ of juicy lime.
- ¼ Tsp white pepper
- 1 shallot or ½ red onion
- 1 green onion
- handful fresh cilantro
- half handful fresh mint
- 1 Tbs cooking oil
- 1 heaping Tbs palm sugar
- 3 Tbs fish sauce
- 2 to 3 Tsp Thai chili flakes

To Serve with
- cucumber
- green lettuce
- warm cooked jasmine rice

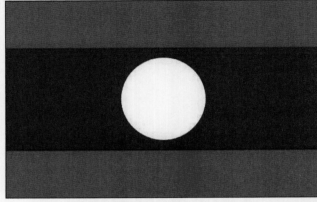

Butter Lettuce for a great wrap.

INSTRUCTIONS:

1. Heat a medium size skillet over medium heat; add uncooked jasmine rice and toast until nice golden brown, about 10 to 15 minutes. Transfer to a mortar or spice grinder and grind toasted rice into your desired fineness

2. In a mixing bowl, combine pork, juice form ½ of juicy lime and white pepper. Mix well and set aside.

3. Meanwhile, slice shallot thinly, chop green onion, cilantro and prepare mint by taking leaves off from stem. Set aside.

4. Heat a wok or large skillet over high heat, add cooking oil. Add marinated pork and cook until all the juices are gone, about 7 to 9 minutes. Remove from heat and add palm sugar into pork when pork is still hot, so it will help palm sugar to resolve easier.

5. In a large mixing bowl, add fish sauce and squeeze fresh juice from 2 juicy limes. Stir with a spoon to combine and add cooked pork along with all of vegetables we prepared easier, Thai chili flakes and toasted jasmine rice powder. (Leave toasted rice powder a bit for garnish later on)

6. Toss everything together until everything is well combined. Transfer to a serving plate and serve with cucumber, green lettuce and warm cooked jasmine rice to your taste.

Piragi

Country: Latvia   **Servings: 6**

INSTRUCTIONS:
- ½ lb bacon rashes diced finely
- 2 brown onions finely diced
- Ground pepper to taste
- 2 Tbs dry instant yeast
- ¼ C warm water
- ¼ C unsalted butter
- ¾ C milk
- 2 Tbs caster sugar, superfine sugar
- 1 egg beaten
- 3½ C plain flour
- 2 Tsp salt
- 1 egg, beaten
- 2 Tbs water

Don't have time to make dough? Biscuit dough works too!

INGREDIENTS:
1. In a heavy non stick pan sauté onions and bacon until the onions are translucent and most of the bacon fat has rendered.
2. Add ground pepper to taste.
3. Leave this mixture to cool completely while you are making the dough. I usually make the bacon/onion mix the day before and leave it in my fridge until I am ready to use it. The bacon mixture is easier to work with when cold. 4. Place yeast and water in a small bowl, put aside for the yeast to activate. It will froth up.
5. In a small saucepan add butter, milk and sugar. Warm over a low heat until butter has melted and sugar has dissolved into the milk.
6. When milk mixture has cooled to lukewarm stir through beaten egg, yeast and water.
7. Place two cups of the plain flour and salt in a large bowl, pour liquid over and stir to combine.
8. Once combined add the remaining flour. Mix until all ingredients have come together, then leave to rest in the bowl for 10 minutes.
9. Once rested turn dough out on to a lightly floured surface and knead until dough is smooth and elastic, about 5 - 10 minutes.
10. Place dough back in to a lightly oiled bowl and cover. Leave dough to raise, around 1½ hours or until doubled in size.
11. Preheat oven 360°F
12. Once dough is ready, start pulling off a walnut size pieces of dough. Work them in to a ball in your hand then tease them out to a circle. Place a tablespoon of the bacon mixture, and bring the edges of the dough together. Seal the bun in a torpedo shape.
13. Place formed buns on a baking tray that has been lined with baking paper. 14. Mix the beaten egg and water together to make an egg wash. Brush egg wash mixture on buns. Place buns in oven and bake until golden, 12-15 minutes.

Country: Libya   **Servings: 6**

INGREDIENTS
- 2 C bread flour
- 2 C whole wheat flour
- 1 packet yeast
- 2 Tsp sugar
- 1 Tsp salt
- ¾ C warm water
- Olive oil

A well-oiled sheet pan will work until instead of a stone pan.

INSTRUCTIONS:
1. Flour Counters
2. In a big, deep bowl add ¾ cups warm water, yeast and sugar and mix together.
3. Leave for 10 mins and let the yeast "activate."
4. Add wheat and white flour and salt to bowl.
5. Mix together to incorporate the salt into the dough.
6. Slowly add water to dough as kneading
7. Knead for 10-15 mins to build the gluten. When the dough forms a ball, sticks together, and the edges of the bowl are "clean" you know you are done. Alternatively you can let your kitchen aid mixer and dough hook knead it for you. It is done when smooth. Cover with a towel and let rest for 20 mins
8. The dough will have risen. Punch down and knead again for an addition 5-8 mins. Cover again and let rest for 30 mins.
9. The dough will rise, Make sure you use a big enough bowl.
10. Clean your counter top very well. Cover in a layer of olive oil for the bread to rest on
11. Preheat oven to 500°F or the highest temperature allowed.
12. Pinch dough into balls and let rest on counter top.
13. Make sure to pat the top of each dough mounds with olive oil. It keeps it moist and adds flavor. Leave mounds for 15 mins to rest.
14. Covering hands in olive oil, pick up a piece of dough flatten in hand before placing on stone
15. Place on stone and in a fanning motion spread dough to make a circle. about 3-4 inches round
16. Allow to bake for 2-3 mins till the edges begin to brown and it puffs up, flip it over for another couple minutes and remove, it will deflate once you remove it from the hot oven.

Country: Madagascar   **Servings: 6**

INGREDIENTS:
- 2¼ cups of flour
- 1½ tsp salt
- 1 tsp curry powder
- 1 tsp baking soda
- ¾ tsp black pepper
- 1½ C water
- ½ C watercress, chopped
- 3 red or green chilies, finely chopped
- 2 green onions, chopped
- 1 tomato, chopped
- oil for frying

Heat the oil to 350 degrees for frying.

INSTRUCTIONS:
1. In a bowl combine all the ingredients except the oil
2. Mix to form a smooth paste, add water slowly as you may not need the entire 1½ cups
3. Pour the oil into a skillet or deep fryer
4. Drop the batter about a tablespoon at a time into the hot oil and fry the fritters turning frequently until golden brown.
5. Remove the fritters and place on a paper towel to remove excess oil
6. Serve hot.

Country: Malaysia   **Servings: 4**

INGREDIENTS/ SUPPLIES:
- 2 tea mugs or cups
- Kettle
- Stainless steel jug for pouring to "pull" the tea
- 2 C boiling water
- 2 black tea bags
- 2 Tbs condensed milk

Teh Tarik literally translates to "Pulled Tea"

INSTRUCTIONS:
1. Place teabags in a mug and pour over boiling water. Steep for a few minutes until tea is dark and intense, then allow to cool for a few more minutes.
2.Add 2 tbsp condensed milk and stir until spoon is clean.

For the adventurous:
- (Caution: Please be careful with hot tea to avoid a burn!)

Pour the tea into a stainless steel jug, then pour into a mug or tea glass. Try to gain as much height as possible while pouring. Repeat until tea is frothy. Serve hot or over plenty of ice

Country: Marshal Islands   **Servings: 6**

INGREDIENTS:
• 2 C short grain rice
• 1 coconut, meat shredded

The simplest recipe in the book! Perfect for a last minute dessert or side.

INSTRUCTIONS
1. Prepare the rice according to package directions. The steamed rice should be a little sticky when steamed
2. Grate the meat of a coconut.
3. When the rice is cool enough to handle, roll them into balls about the size of a golf ball
4. Roll them in the grated coconut and serve with fish or chicken

Country: Mexico   **Servings: 6**

INGREDIENTS:
Cake:
- ¼ C caramel topping
- 1 box Chocolate fudge cake mix
- 1 C water
- ½ C vegetable oil
- 3 eggs

Flan:
- 1 can (14 oz) sweetened condensed milk
- 1 C evaporated milk
- 4 eggs

Make your own Dulce de leche by adding a can on sweetened condensed milk (unopened) to a Crockpot full of water. Leave on low for 12 hours

INSTRUCTIONS:
1.Heat oven to 350°F. Spray 12-cup fluted tube cake pan with cooking spray. Pour and spread caramel topping in bottom of pan.

2. In large bowl, beat cake mix, water, oil and 3 eggs with electric mixer on medium speed 2 minutes, scraping bowl occasionally. Pour batter over caramel topping in pan.

3. In blender, place Flan ingredients. Cover; blend on high speed about 20 seconds or until smooth. Slowly pour mixture evenly over batter. (Flan mixture will mix with batter, but they will separate during baking, forming 1 layer of cake and 1 layer of flan.) Spray piece of foil with cooking spray, and place sprayed side down over top of pan; cover tightly.

4. Place cake pan in large roasting pan; add 1 inch of hot water to roasting pan.

5. Bake 1 hour 20 minutes to ensure cake AND flan layer bake completely (toothpick inserted in center of cake will come out clean). Remove cake pan from water bath to cooling rack; remove foil. Cool at room temperature 1 hour. Refrigerate in pan, uncovered, 2 hours.

6. Remove from refrigerator; run thin metal spatula around outer and inside edges of pan to loosen cake. Place serving plate upside down on cake pan; turn plate and pan over. Remove pan. Spoon any remaining caramel from pan over top of cake. Store loosely covered in refrigerator.

Country: Morocco   **Servings: 4**

INGREDIENTS:
- 2 Tbs ras el hanout
- 1½ C Greek-style natural yogurt
- 1 Tbs lemon juice
- 6 skinless chicken breast fillets, cut into 1/2 IN chunks
- 2 small garlic cloves, crushed
- 1 Tsp hot paprika
- 1 Tbs butter
- 8 ½ oz tomato sauce
- a pinch of sugar
- 6 flat breads
- 1 pack mint, leaves only
- 1 pack coriander, roughly chopped

Ras El Hanout is equal parts:
- **Paprika**
- **Coriander**
- **Ginger**
- **Pinch of curry**

It means, "head of the shop"

INSTRUCTIONS:

1. If using bamboo skewers, soak in water for 1 hour. Mix the ras el hanout with 1 C yogurt, a pinch of salt and the lemon juice then stir in the chicken. Marinate for 30 minutes if you have time. Mix the remaining yogurt with half the crushed garlic and seasoning and set aside to serve.

2. Preheat the barbecue or grill. Thread the chicken onto skewers. Cook the chicken skewers for 12-15 minutes, turning regularly, then allow to rest for 3-5 minutes.

3. Meanwhile make a quick tomato sauce. Cook the remaining garlic and paprika in the butter for 30 seconds, add the tomato sauce, sugar and season. Simmer gently for 10 minutes.

4. Heat the flat breads for 1 minute each side to warm them through. Serve the chicken with the garlic yogurt, the charred flat breads, the spicy sauce and a generous handful of mint and coriander.

Country: Nepal   **Servings: 4**

INGREDIENTS:
• 2 lbs boneless chicken breasts or 2 lbs chicken thighs, cut into 1-inch cubes
• bamboo skewer, soaked for at least 30 minutes
• melted butter, for basting

MARINADE:
• 1 Tsp curry powder
• 1 Tbs oil
• 3 fresh red chilies, minced
• 1 Tbs finely minced fresh cilantro
• 1 Tbs finely chopped lemon grass or 1 Tsp grated lime zest
• ½ Tbs turmeric
• ¼ Tsp grated nutmeg
• ¼ Tsp szechuan pepper
• ½ C yogurt
• 1 Tsp garlic paste
• 1 Tsp ginger paste
• salt and pepper

Use the Turkish Flat bread from page 158 to make a great wrap!

INSTRUCTIONS:
1. In a blender, process all marinating ingredients into a smooth paste.
2. Marinate chicken cubes in marinade for overnight in the refrigerator.
3. Pat dry marinated chicken pieces and thread on with soaked bamboo skewers.
4. Grill to the desired doneness, frequently turning and basting with the melted butter.
5. Serve hot with rice pilaf and stir-fried vegetables

Country: The Netherlands   **Servings: 8**

INGREDIENTS:
- 1 Tbs active dry yeast
- 1 C lukewarm water
- 3 C all purpose flour
- 2/3 C whole wheat flour
- 2 ½ Tbs granulated sugar
- ½ Tbs sea salt
- 3 tablespoons unsalted butter, room temperature
- 1 egg
- 2.6 ounces sunflower seeds
- 2 carrots, peeled and grated

They taste great with honey and butter!

INSTRUCTIONS:
1.In a small bowl, sprinkle the yeast over the warm water. Stir to combine and allow to sit until frothy, 5-10 minutes. 2.In the bowl of a stand mixer fitted with a dough hook or a large bowl, combine the flours, sugar, and salt. Mix in the yeast with water and butter until the dough comes together.

3.On a lightly floured surface, knead the dough until smooth and elastic. If too dry, add a little more water. If too sticky, add a little more flour.

4.Transfer to an oiled bowl, turning to coat, cover, and allow to rest until doubled, about 1 hour.

5.Line a large baking sheet with parchment.

Place the risen dough on a floured surface and form a well in the center. Crack an egg into the well and add the sunflower seeds and carrots.

6.Pull the edges of the dough together over the filling and seal to close.

7.Use a large knife or dough scraper to cut the ball of dough into small pieces. Fold, cut again, and scrape the dough back into a ball to mix the ingredients. Divide the dough into 6 pieces and arrange on the prepared baking sheet.

8.Cover and allow to rise until puffed, about 1 hour. 9.Preheat oven to 430°F. Bake the rolls in the preheated oven until golden, about 15 minutes. Allow to cool on wire rack before serving.

Country: New Zealand   **Servings:6**

INGREDIENTS
• 6 egg whites, at room temperature
• 1½ C granulated/caster sugar
• pinch salt
• 3 Tsp cornflour/cornstarch
• 1 Tsp white vinegar
• 1 Tsp vanilla essence
• 1 C cream, for whipping
• strawberries or other fresh berries,

Pavlova is named after a Russian dancer.

INSTRUCTIONS
1. Preheat oven to 300°F
2. In a large, clean bowl, whisk together the egg whites and salt until stiff peaks form.
3. Gradually add sugar, 1/4 of a cup at a time and whisk after each addition for about 1 minute. Whisk until sugar has dissolved. To test to see if it's dissolved, gently rub a little bit of the meringue mixture between your fingers. If it's grainy, keep whisking.
4. After the last of the sugar has been added, whisk on high for 3 minutes. The mixture should be very thick and glossy.
5. Combine the cornflour/cornstarch, vinegar and vanilla essence in a very small bowl.
6. Add to the meringue mixture and whisk until just combined.
7. Line a 12" round pizza tray with a piece of baking paper/ parchment paper cut into a circle.
8. Start scooping out the meringue mixture, forming a circle roughly 8-9" in diameter.
9. Use a spatula, to gently start shaping your Pavlova. Start at the bottom and gently make nice neat lines moving toward the top of the Pavlova (see image).
10. Reduce oven temperature to 250°F and place Pavlova in the oven on the middle shelf.
11. Cook for 1 hour to 1 hour and 15 minutes. Turn on oven light to see the Pavlova. The Pavlova should be lightly browned. If you to, quickly open the oven door and touch the Pavlova. It should be dry to the touch.
12. Turn off the oven, and leave the Pavlova in the oven with the door closed for 3 hours until the Pavlova is cooled down.
13. To serve, whip the cream, and gently spoon into the center of the Pavlova. Top with fresh berries.

Country: Nicaragua   **Servings: 4**

INGREDIENTS:
- 1 package (14-16 oz) small dried red beans, such as Central American red beans (**not kidney beans**). 3 c cooked beans needed for recipe
- 2½ C red bean cooking liquid
- 2 C uncooked long grain white rice
- 1/3 C vegetable or canola oil
- ½ C onion finely chopped
- 3 Tsp salt, divided

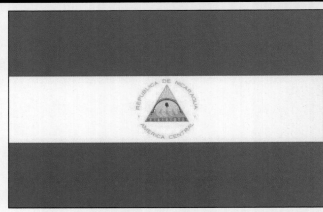

Use an Instant Pot for perfect rice every time.

INSTRUCTIONS:
1. Pick through beans to remove any debris and rinse well with water
2. Place beans in a large pot and add enough water to cover by 3-4 inches
3. Bring to a boil
4. Reduce heat to low or medium-low to keep at a slow boil
5. Boil gently, partially covered for about 1 1/2 hours or until beans are tender, but firm "al dente". Check after 1 hour to ensure too much water hasn't evaporated. Add more if needed. Add 2 teaspoons salt during last 30 minutes of cooking time. Once cooked, set pot aside at room temperature and keep beans in their cooking liquid until ready to use.
6. In a wide saucepan with about 2" sides, heat oil over medium heat
7. Add chopped onion and saute for 2-3 minutes, until slightly softened
8. Measure out 3 cups of cooked beans, removing from bean liquid with slotted spoon. Add to oil and onion.
9. Immediately add 2 1/2 cups of bean cooking liquid, 2 cups uncooked rice, and 1 teaspoon salt
10. Bring to a quick boil and then reduce heat to low
11. Cover and cook on low for about 20 minutes or until rice is cooked
12. Adjust salt as needed

Suya

Country: Nigeria   **Servings: 4**

INGREDIENTS:
- 1 lb sirloin steak cut into 1 inch cubes
- 1 small onion
- 2 Tbs peanut butter, unsalted
- 1 Tbs tomato paste
- 1 Tbs olive oil
- 2 Tsp All Spice
- ½ Tsp salt
- ¼ Tsp crushed red pepper
- ¼ Tsp powdered ginger
- Cooking spray

Use high fat ground beef if you're short on time.

INSTRUCTIONS:

1. In the bowl of a food processor, grate the onion until it's finely chopped. Add the peanut butter, tomato paste, olive oil, all spice, salt, crushed red pepper and

powdered ginger. Continue to blend until the mixture is well combined and smooth.

2. Transfer the sauce from the blender to a large bowl. Add the beef to the sauce and toss to coat. Cover and refrigerate for 20 minutes to allow the beef to marinade.

3. When ready to grill, thread the beef onto wooden or metal skewers. Pour any leftover marinade on top of the beef kabobs.

4. Preheat the grill to medium-high heat, and grease the grill with cooking spray.

5. Cook on the preheated grill, flipping once, until meat is browned, about 10-15 minutes.

Kalbi (North Korean Short Rib)

Country: North Korea   **Servings: 6**

Ingredients:
- 4-6 pounds beef short ribs
- 1 cup soy sauce
- 1 cup beef broth
- 2 tablespoons rice vinegar
- 1/2 cup dark brown sugar
- 1/2 tablespoon black pepper
- 1 tablespoon sesame oil
- 5 cloves garlic, minced
- 1 tablespoon ginger, minced
- 1 medium yellow onion, thinly sliced
- 1 teaspoon red pepper flakes (optional) or 2 tablespoons Gochujang

To finish:
- 2 tablespoons cornstarch
- 1/4 cup cold water
- 2-3 green onions, sliced on the diagonal into 1-inch pieces for garnish
- 1 teaspoon toasted sesame seeds for garnish

Serve with white rice.

Instructions:
1. Arrange the short ribs in the bottom of a slow cooker, then sprinkle with the thinly sliced onion.
2. Mix together the soy sauce, beef broth, rice vinegar, brown sugar, black pepper, sesame oil, garlic, ginger, and red pepper flakes, then pour over the short ribs.
3. Cover the slow cooker and cook on low heat for 6-8 hours or on high heat for 3-4 hours.
4. When almost ready to serve, whisk the cornstarch into the cold water and pour into the slow cooker, stirring to combine with the sauce and juices from the meat. Cover and cook another 20 minutes, until the liquid has thickened slightly.

Country: Norway   **Servings: 6**

INGREDIENTS:
• 1 lbs lean ground beef
• ½ lbs ground pork
• 2 egg, lightly beaten
• 1½ C bread crumbs
• 1 C whole milk
• 2 Tsp salt
• 1 Tsp ground pepper
• 1½ Tsp ground nutmeg
• ½ Tsp ground ginger
• ½ Tsp allspice
• 8 Tbs (1 stick or 1/2 cup) butter; divided
• ½ C flour
• 4 C beef stock
• ¼ cup sour cream
• Salt and pepper, to taste
• Lingonberry jam or Red Currant jelly

These meatballs freeze very well, perfect for dinner the next week!

INSTRUCTIONS:
1. In a large bowl, add the milk and bread crumbs. Allow the milk to be absorbed by the bread crumbs and then whisk in the eggs and spices (salt, pepper, nutmeg, ginger, and allspice). Mix until incorporated. Then add the ground meats and with your finger tips, lightly mix the milk-bread crumb mixture into the meat mixture until well combined being mindful not to compact the mixture tightly.
2. Form the meat into 2-oz balls (about the size of golf balls). Into a large skillet or Dutch oven over medium heat, melt half the butter (4 tbsp) and lightly fry the meatballs, turning until they are browned on all sides, but not cooked through. You may need to work in two batches. Once all the meatballs have been browned remove them from pan and set aside while you prepare the gravy.
3. Into the same skillet or Dutch oven you cooked the meatballs in, add the remaining 4 tbsp butter over medium-low heat. Stir in the flour to make a roux and allow to cook for a minute – the roux will still be blonde in color. Then slowly whisk the broth into the roux. Once the roux is incorporated into the broth, turn the heat up to medium and add the meatballs back into the pan and cook for about 20 minutes over medium heat until the meatballs are cooked through. The gravy should come to a boil and thicken as the meatballs simmer. If the gravy is too thick, add a little more broth (or water) to thin it to your desired consistency. If the gravy is too thin you can cook a little longer allowing the sauce to reduce to your desired consistency.
4. Once your desired consistency is reached, remove the pan from the heat and whisk in the sour cream. Taste the sauce and adjust your seasonings to your desired tastes.
5. Serve with mashed potatoes, seasonal vegetables and Lingonberry jam

Aloo Gosht

Country: Pakistan   **Servings: 6**

INGREDIENTS:
- 1 lb stew beef (could also use goat or lamb)
- 3 Tb cooking oil, divided
- 1 large onion, thinly sliced
- 1 stick cinnamon
- 1 black cardamom pod
- 5 black peppercorns
- 5 cloves
- 3 cloves garlic, peeled and grated
- 1 inch ginger, peeled and grated
- 1 Tsp red chili powder
- 1 Tsp coriander powder
- ½ Tsp turmeric
- 3 Roma tomatoes, diced
- 1 Tsp salt (or to taste)
- 3 medium red potatoes, peeled and diced into large chunks
- 3 green Thai chilies, thickly sliced
- 1 handful cilantro, roughly chopped

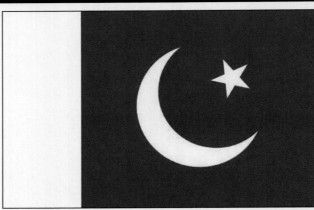

Check out the goats bone broth recipe on page 182!

INSTRUCTIONS:
1. Heat a tbsp of the oil on high in a heavy-bottomed pot. Season the stew beef with salt and pepper and brown. Remove to a plate.
2. Lower heat to medium or medium high, and add two more tbsp oil (making sure to scrape up any brown bits from the pot). Fry the onions, stirring, until they start to turn golden.
3. Add whole spices (cinnamon, black cardamom, black peppercorns and cloves) and cook, stirring, until fragrant (about a minute or two). Add garlic and ginger and cook, stirring for a minute or two, then the ground spices (red chili, coriander, turmeric) and cook, stirring for a minute and being careful not to burn. 4. Add tomatoes and salt (stir well at this point to de glaze anything stuck to the pot) and cook until the tomatoes are well broken down and the oil starts to separate from the sauce.
3. Add the beef back into the pot along with 1.5 - 2 cups water. Bring to a boil, then reduce to a simmer and cook, covered, until beef is very tender

Country: Panama   **Servings: 8**

INGREDIENTS:
• Water
• 2 cinnamon sticks
• 2 oz of dried hibiscus
flowers
• ginger to taste
• ½ Tsp cloves
• 1½ C of cane sugar

Find hibiscus flowers on Amazon.

INSTRUCTIONS:
1. Boil everything together for a few minutes until sugar is dissolved and flowers expanded.
2. Strain and serve over ice

Peruvian Chicken

Country: Peru   **Servings: 4**

INGREDIENTS:
Chicken:
- 3 lb chicken, fresh or defrosted
- 3 Tbs paprika
- 2 Tbs ground cumin
- 1½ Tbs minced garlic
- 2 Tbs lime juice
- 4 Tbs canola oil
- 1 Tsp freshly ground black pepper
- ½ Tsp Kosher salt
- ¼ C chopped cilantro for garnish
- ½ C water to add to Instant Pot only

Green Sauce:
- 5 jalapeños, seeds removed if you don't like spice also remove veins
- 1 C cilantro about a bunch
- 1 small yellow onion
- 1 large garlic clove
- 1/3 C feta cheese or queso fresco
- 1 Tbs lime juice
- 1/3 C canola oil
- kosher salt to taste

Don't have an instant pot? Cook in a Crockpot on high for 4 hours, and then broil for 5 mins.

INSTRUCTIONS:

Instant Pot:
1. Marinate chicken in spice mixture for one hour, or ideally overnight.
2. Turn Instant Pot on saute and heat 2 tablespoons of canola oil until it shimmers. Brown chicken on all sides.
3. Remove chicken. Add 1/2 cup water to the Instant Pot and place chicken on trivet in pot.
4. Cook on manual setting and cook 6 minutes per pound, or 18 minutes for a 3lb chicken. NPR (natural pressure release) for 10 minutes.
5. Garnish with chopped parsley and serve alongside fries and green sauce

Oven:
1. Marinate chicken in spice mixture for one hour, or ideally overnight. 2. Preheat oven to 350°F.
3. Place dutch oven on stove over medium-high heat. Heat 2 tablespoons of canola oil until it shimmers. Brown chicken on all sides.
4. Cook in oven with lid on for 80 minutes. Remove lid and cook for another 10-20 minutes. Internal temperature should be 165°F.

Green Sauce:
Place everything but oil and salt in blender and pulse to chop. Stream in canola oil until it's blended smoothly. As some feta is more salty than others taste for seasoning and add kosher salt as needed.

Country: Philippines

Servings: 4

INGREDIENTS:
• 1 C Brown Sugar
• 1 C Water
• 1/4 Tsp Banana Essence (or vanilla)
• Sago
• Gulaman
• Ice Cubes

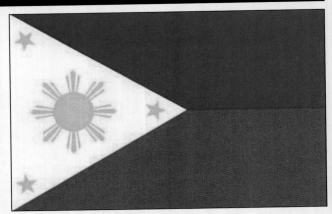

Check out page 188 for gulaman and sago recipes.

INSTRUCTIONS:
1. To make the syrup for Sago at Gulaman, first set a small pot over medium heat. Then you'll want to put in 1 cup of brown sugar. Followed by 1 cup of water. And ¼ a teaspoon of banana essence. Continuously stir everything together until the brown sugar is fully dissolved.
2. Once its fully dissolved, just gather the following ingredients: water, gulaman cut into cubes, ice cubes, and sago pearls.
3. Just put in as much sago and gulaman as you like. Depending on how sweet you like yours, you can adjust the ratio of the syrup to water that you add in. Then drop in a couple ice cubes and stir.

Szarlotka

Country: Poland   **Servings: 6**

INGREDIENTS:

For the filling
- 5-6 Granny Smith apples, cored, peeled and chopped
- 1 Tsp cornstarch
- ½ Tsp cinnamon
- pinch of nutmeg
- pinch of cloves
- ½ C sugar

For the crust
- 1 C flour (substitute gluten free flour if you like)
- ¼ Tsp baking powder
- ¼ C sugar
- 2 small organic egg yolks
- 1 Tbs sour cream or Greek yogurt
- ⅓ C cold butter
- ½ Tsp vanilla

For the meringue
- 3 small egg whites (use the two from the yolk plus you'll need 1 more white)
- 3 Tbs sugar

This uses a French Meringue, the easiest of the 3 styles of meringue.

INSTRUCTIONS:

For the filling
1. In a pan over medium heat add the apple, sugar, spices and 1 tablespoon of water. Saute for 15-20 minutes or until the apples become softer.
2. Take a potato masher and mash the apples.
3. In a cup, combine 1 tablespoon of water and the cornstarch. Mix until completely dissolved.
4. Add the cornstarch mixture to the apple mash and mix in.
5. Remove from heat and set aside.

For the crust
1. In a bowl combine all the ingredients until a cookie dough consistency is achieved. Form into a ball.
2. Place the crust ball in the fridge for 30 minutes.
3. Remove the ball from the fridge and shred it with a cheese shredder.
4. Evenly press the shredded crust into an 8″ or 9″ square pan covered with parchment paper.
5. With a fork prick the crust in several places so as to prevent it from rising.
6. Bake in an oven at 360°F until it starts to just turn golden color.
7. Remove from the oven and allow to cool on the counter for a few minutes. 8. While the crust is cooling whip the egg whites.

For the meringue
1. With an electric mixer, whip the egg whites until peaks form.
2. Add 3 tablespoons of sugar and continue to whip until incorporated.

To make the cake
1. Spread the apple pie filling onto the crust and then top with the meringue.
2. Reduce the heat in the oven to 240°F (This is important!)
3. Bake the cake at 240°F for 30-40 minutes or until the meringue turns a nice golden color.
4. Remove from the oven and allow to cool.
5. You can serve this cake topped with whip cream, ice cream, creme fraiche or just as it is!

Portuguese Creamy Chicken

Country: Portugal   **Servings: 4**

INGREDIENTS:
- 2 chicken breasts, cut into steaks
- 1 C of heavy cream
- 3 cloves of garlic
- 1 Tsp of mustard/Ground pepper (to taste)
- Salt (to taste)
- Olive oil (to taste)

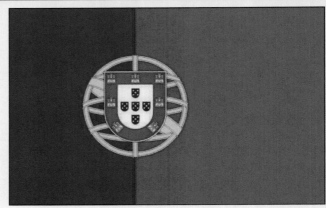

Pair with Arroz Con Queso for a quick meal!

INSTRUCTIONS:
1. Season the steaks with the minced garlic, salt and pepper.
2. Heat a frying pan with olive oil (to taste) and fry the steaks.
3. Add the mustard and cream to the frying pan.
4. Cook until the sauce thickens and serve immediately.

Country: Romania   **Servings: 2**

INGREDIENTS:
- 1¾ C all-purpose (plain) flour
- 2¼ Tsp active dry yeast OR 2 teaspoons instant yeast
- 2 Tb sugar
- ⅛ Tsp salt
- 1 large egg, room temperature
- 3 Tb melted butter
- ½ C milk, lukewarm temperature
- Melted butter (For brushing the rolling pin)
- Sugar (for topping the cake)

For the topping:
- Approximately ½ C sugar

Pro tip: fill with amazing toppings like ice cream or nutella!

INSTRUCTIONS:
1. If you are using active dry yeast, add ½ teaspoon sugar to lukewarm milk and set aside for 5-10 minutes until it proofs
2. You can use the other yeast types directly along with the flour.
3. In a large bowl combine, flour, sugar and salt. To this add egg, milk, melted butter, and yeast. Stir the mixture until it comes together to form a dough, and then knead for about five minutes.
4. It will be sticky. Don't be tempted to add any flour. Grease your hand if needed.
5. Transfer to a well greased container
6. Allow the dough to rise for 60 minutes at room temperature until doubled in volume
7. Prepare the rolling pins by covering them with aluminum foil, do at least two or three layers, to protect the pins from burning in the oven.
8. Brush them with melted butter.
9. The dough will have risen after 60 minutes.
10. Punch down the dough and divide into 4 equal parts
11. On a well floured surface spread one portion of the dough
12. Shape into ⅙ inch thick square-shaped sheet.
13. Using a pizza cutter cut the dough into a long ribbons of about ½ inch wide
14. Wrap one end of the dough strip around the spit/rolling pin, tucking in the end so the dough doesn't unwind.
15. Keep the dough very thin (under ¼ inch) as you stretch and wind it on the rolling pin. Then roll the whole thing slightly on the counter top to flatten it/press it together.
16. Brush with melted butter and roll in sugar
17. Place in roasting pan and bake in a preheated oven (375°F) for 25 minutes. Gently (with oven mitts) turn the rolling pin every 5-7 mins until it is golden brown on all sides.
18. When cake is done roll it in sugar again
19. Tap the mold on a table top to release the cake and set it up right to cool.

133

Country: Russia   **Servings: 4**

INGREDIENTS:
- 1½ C plus 2 Tb vegetable oil
- 2 C thinly sliced cabbage
- ½ C finely chopped onion
- ½ pound ground beef
- 3/4 Tsp dried dill
- ½ Tsp garlic powder
- ¾ Tsp salt
- ¼ Tsp black pepper
- 1 (16.3-ounce) package refrigerated flaky layer biscuits

Pro Tip: Grab the biscuit dough without butter for easier handling.

INSTRUCTIONS:
1. In a large skillet over medium heat, heat 2 tablespoons oil; saute cabbage and onion 5 to 7 minutes or until cabbage is wilted. Place cabbage mixture in a bowl and set aside.

2. In the same skillet over medium-high heat, cook ground beef 5 minutes or until browned, breaking up any clumps as it cooks; drain liquid. Add cabbage mixture back into skillet. Stir in dill, garlic powder, salt, and pepper; mix well.

3. Gently pull apart each biscuit in half, making 16 flat circles. With your fingers, flatten each circle into a 3 inch round diameter. Place 1 tablespoon of meat mixture into center of each piece of dough. Fold dough in half over the meat, forming a half moon shape, and firmly pinch edges to seal.

4. In a deep skillet over medium-high heat, heat remaining 1-1/2 cups oil until hot but not smoking. It should be about 350°F Place stuffed dough in oil and cook in batches 1 to 2 minutes per side or until golden brown. Remove with a slotted spoon to a paper towel-lined platter. Serve warm.

Country: Samoa Islands   **Servings: 6**

INGREDIENTS:
- 1 can (10 ounces) Coconut Milk
- 3 Tbs sweetened condensed milk
- ½ C sugar
- ½ Tbs Corn Starch
- 1 12-pack Sweet Dinner Rolls

Top with shredded coconut for some crunch!

INSTRUCTIONS:
1. Preheat oven to 350°F. Separate dinner rolls and place evenly in a baking tray or skillet.
2. In a pot, bring coconut milk, condensed milk, cornstarch, and sugar over to a boil then turn to low heat until sugar is dissolved and mixture thickens (about 5 minutes).
3. Use a fork to poke holes in rolls (this will help the bread soak up the liquid mixture), then evenly pour coconut mixture over the rolls.
4. Place tray in oven for 6-8 minutes until tops are a rich golden brown and enjoy!

Musaka

Country: Serbia   **Servings: 6**

INGREDIENTS:
- ¼ C olive oil
- 4 lbs russet potatoes
- 1 medium onion chopped
- 1 lb ground beef or pork
- salt and pepper to taste

Topping:
- 4 eggs
- 1 C yogurt or sour cream
- 2 C milk
- salt and pepper to taste

This recipe is similar to moussaka, a Greek dish made with eggplant.

INSTRUCTIONS:

1. Peel the russet potatoes and slice into 1/4 inch (no larger) thick circles.

2. In a large pan, drizzle olive oil over medium heat. Add onions and cook, stirring often, until lightly browned. Stir in ground meat, breaking up with a spoon, and season with salt and pepper. Continue cooking and breaking apart the meat until browned.

3. Preheat oven to 400 degrees F and grease a 9x13 inch baking dish with olive oil.

4. Layer half of the sliced potatoes, about 2 layers, on the bottom of the prepared baking dish. Season with salt and pepper. Cover with the cooked ground meat. Layer the remaining potatoes, another 2 layers.

5. In a medium bowl, whisk together eggs, yogurt, milk, salt, and pepper. Pour evenly over the potatoes until it is right below the top layer. Bake in preheated oven until potatoes are tender and top is golden brown, about 1 hour. Broil, if desired, to crisp the top further.

6. Let sit for 10 minutes before slicing and serving.

Singapore Chili Crab

INGREDIENTS:
- 2 live medium sized crabs
- 2 tomatoes
- 2 Tbsp tomato ketchup
- 2 Tbs tamarind
- 2 Tbs veg oil
- ½ Tsp salt
- 1 Tsp white sugar (if needed)
- ½ C water
- 1 egg, lightly beaten
- small handful chopped coriander (cilantro)
- small handful chives, chopped

Paste:
- 1 medium onion
- 3 red Thai (or any bird's eye) chillies
- 3 cloves garlic
- 2″ fresh ginger
- 2 Tbs taucheo (soybean paste) or use same amount of hoisin sauce (found in supermarkets)

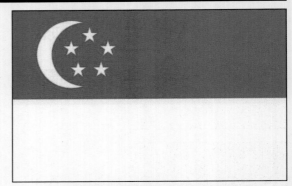

Use Blue Crab or even crab legs if Dungeness isn't available.

INSTRUCTIONS:
1. Clean and chop crab.
2. Heat oil in a large wok and fry the paste ingredients until fragrant, about 2 minutes.
3. Add the tomatoes, water, ketchup, tamarind then crabs and give it all a good stir. Cover and cook for 8-10 minutes until the crabs are done.
4. Taste and add more salt if needed. If you find the sauce too spicy, add some sugar.
5. Add the egg and gently mix it in for 20 seconds, and turn the heat off and take the wok off the heat. You want wisps of it, not scrambled bits.
6. Garnish with the herbs and serve with rice.

Country: South Africa   **Servings: 4**

INGREDIENTS:

Tripe:
- 1.5 lb tripe, pre-cooked and cubed
- 1 Tsp salt
- 1 Tb lemon juice

Tomato sauce:
- 4 Tb oil
- 1 onion, finely chopped
- 2 carrots, diced
- 2 stalks of celery, finely chopped
- 1 can tomato paste
- 1 can chopped tomatoes
- 1 C dry wine
- 2 Tb sugar

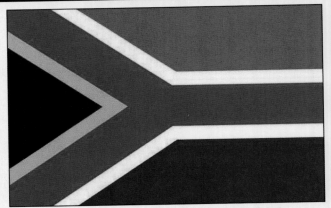

This dish is a favorite of Nelson Mandela.

INSTRUCTIONS:

Tripe:

1. Wash and rinse tripe thoroughly.

2. Place in cold water, add salt and lemon juice.

3. Bring to boil and simmer gently for 2 hours or until tender.

To make sauce:

1. Heat oil and add remaining ingredients and simmer for 15 minutes.

2. Drain tripe and add to tomato sauce.

3. Cook for an additional 20 minutes.

4. Serve hot with rice.

Bulgogi Jeongol

Country: South Korea   **Servings: 4**

INGREDIENTS:
For the Sauce
- 10 to 12 cloves garlic, finely chopped
- 6 Tbs soy sauce
- 3 Tbs fish sauce
- 5 Tbs sugar
- 4 Tbs red wine (any kinds will work)
- ¼ Tsp black pepper

For the Meat & Veggies
- 1 lb thinly sliced beef rib eye or skirt steak
- 14 oz udon noodles
- ½ large onion, sliced
- 1 bundle of Mexican green onions or 2 bundles of green onions, cut into 2-inch long pieces
- 1 block soft or medium soft tofu, sliced into ½-inch thick
- 1 lb mushrooms, sliced or/and cut into bite sizes if needed
- handful crown daisy (You can also use napa cabbage, bok choy, kale, spinach or/and swiss chard)
- 3 C water
- sesame seeds

A Hot Pot is perfect throw together meal for a crowd.

INSTRUCTIONS:

1. Combine all ingredients for the sauce in a medium size mixing bowl and stir well until sugar has completely dissolved.

2. Bring thinly sliced beef and pour half of the sauce. Mix well and set aside to marinate the beef. You could marinate for over night but it's not necessary. Let it marinate while you're preparing the veggies and other ingredients will be enough time!

3. Drain noodles and rinse under hot water for 1 to 2 minutes then drain.

4. Spread sliced onion on bottom of the shallow large pot. Arrange the rest of the vegetables, tofu and noodles in the pot and leave the center.

5. Place the bulgogi in the center and pour the rest of the sauce around, but not on top of the bulgogi. Pour water from the side of the pot and sprinkle some sesame seeds right on top to garnish. Cover with a lid. We usually serve this jeongol (hot pot) to the dinner table, and eat while it's cooking. So if you have a portable gas stove, please do so! It's so much more fun!

6. Bring it to boil over high heat and when it starts boil, start move around the bulgogi in the middles so the beef will cook evenly. Keep boiling for 5 minutes or until bulgogi is fully cooked and vegetables are soften. It's ready to eat! Enjoy!

Country: Spain   **Servings: 6**

INGREDIENTS:
- 2 Tbs olive oil
- 7 oz chorizo
- 3 garlic cloves
- 1 onion
- 1 red bell pepper
- 1 large tomato
- 10 oz chicken thigh fillets
- 1½ C paella rice
- 3½ C chicken broth
- 1 Tsp saffron threads (or 1/2 tsp turmeric powder)
- 12- 16 medium / large prawns , whole (shell on)
- 12 large mussels

Paella can be made with squid, rabbit, and clams!

INSTRUCTIONS:
1. Heat 1 tbsp oil in a large skillet over high heat. Add chorizo and cook until browned. Remove with a slotted spoon.
2. Heat remaining oil. Add garlic and onion, cook for 3 minutes or until translucent. Add bell pepper and cook until softened. Add tomato and cook for 1 minute to soften.
3. Add chicken and squid. Cook until chicken is lightly browned all over but still raw inside.
4. Add rice and mix until the grains are coated in oil.
5. Add in most of the chorizo (reserve some for garnish).
6. Add chicken broth and saffron, stir once, then leave until it starts simmering. Turn the heat down slightly to medium high so it is simmering energetically but not rapidly for 3 minutes, then turn the heat down to medium. Do not stir!
7. Cook for another 7 minutes (no stirring!) - There should still be plenty of liquid but you can see rice on the surface. Shove the prawns into the rice, pushing it in so they are mostly immersed, then push the mussels in so they are partially immersed. The mussels will leech liquid.
8. Cook for 5 - 8 minutes or until prawns are opaque, mussels are open and most of the liquid has evaporated. Discard any that do not open.
9. Scatter over reserve chorizo - residual heat will warm through

Country: Switzerland   **Servings: 4**

INGREDIENTS:
• ¾ C Gruyère Cheese,
• ¾ C Swiss Emmental Cheese,
• ¼ C Appenzeller Cheese,
• 5oz Dry White Wine,
• 2 Tsp Corn Starch,
• 1 Clove Garlic, minced,
• Pinch of Nutmeg,
• Salt and pepper for seasoning.

For dipping/eating with:
• A loaf of crusty bread, cubed
• Gherkins
• Apples
• Pears
• Pickled Onions
• Pineapple

Be creative with what you dip! This is great for trying new flavors out.

INSTRUCTIONS:
1. Grate the cheese and mix together. Prep all your ingredients for dipping before you start as the fondue needs to be served immediately as soon as it is ready.
2. Add the wine, garlic and cornstarch into a large saucepan and heat on a medium heat until the mixture begins to thicken.
3. Add the cheese and stir until it is melted and thin. Season with the nutmeg, salt and pepper and transfer into a fondue pot which is heated. Serve and eat immediately.
Note: The fondue should be kept in the fondue pot at a temperature where it is still liquidy, but never bubbling.

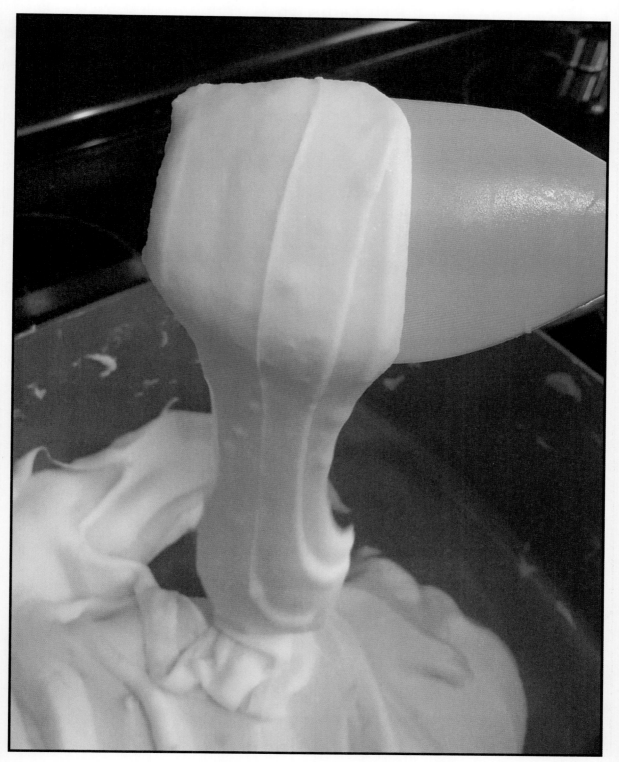

Country: Taiwan **Servings: 4**

INGREDIENTS:
- 1½ lbs Flank Steak
- ¼ C cornstarch
- 2 Tbs Olive Oil
- ½ Tbs mince Garlic
- ¾ C Soy Sauce
- ¾ C Water
- ¾ C Brown Sugar
- 1 C grated Carrots
- Green onions, for garnish

Mongolian Beef is actually a Taiwanese dish! Mongolian barbecue was created by the Taiwanese comedian and restaurateur Wu Zhaonan

INSTRUCTIONS:
1. Cut flank steak into thin strips. In a ziplock bag add flank steak pieces and cornstarch. Shake to coat.
2. Add olive oil, minced garlic, soy sauce, water, brown sugar and carrots to slow cooker. Stir ingredients. Add coated flank steak and stir again until coated in the sauce.
3. Cook for high 2-3 hours or on low 4-5 hours until cooked throughout and tender. Can serve over rice and garnish with green onions.

Country: Thailand   **Servings: 2**

INGREDIENTS:
• 1½ C uncooked short-grain white rice
• 2 C water
• ½ Tsp salt
• 15oz can full fat coconut milk
• 1 C palm sugar
• ½ Tsp cardamom
• 2 mangoes, peeled and diced
• ½ Tsp mint leaves

Make sure to get the yellow mangoes instead of the red and green mangoes.

INSTRUCTIONS:

1. In pressure cooker, combine rice, water, and salt. Set to high pressure for 5 minutes, then when time is up, let pressure naturally release for 5 minutes then release all remaining pressure.

2. While rice is cooking, combine coconut milk, sugar, and cardamom in a small bowl.

3. When rice has finished cooking, add coconut milk mixture to pot and stir until sugar is dissolved. Remove pot from base and place in the fridge for 20-30 minutes or until cooled.

4. To serve, scoop cooled rice onto plate, top with diced mangoes, and sprinkle with crushed mint.

Country: Turkey   **Servings: 4**

INGREDIENTS:
Dough
• ½ lb uncooked store-bought organic pizza dough
Topping
• ½ sweet red pepper, cored, cut into chunks
• 1 shallot, halved
• 2 garlic cloves, peeled
• ½ oz fresh parsley leaves with some stem
• 7 oz ground lamb or ground beef
• 1 Tsp smoked paprika/ground allspice
• ½ Tsp ground cumin/Aleppo-style pepper/ground cinnamon/cayenne pepper/salt
• 4 Tbs tomato paste
• 2 Tbs Private Reserve Greek extra virgin olive oil
• Lemon wedges for later

If you can't find lamb, ground beef works!

INSTRUCTIONS:
1. Heat oven to 450°F. Adjust oven rack to the middle.
2. Prepare the meat mixture. In the large bowl of a food processor, fitted with blade, add red peppers, shallot, garlic, and parsley. Pulse a few times to chop. To the mixture, add ground lamb (or beef). Season with spices and salt. Add tomato paste and extra virgin olive oil. Now pulse again until well-combined (about 8 to 10 pulses.)
3. Prepare two large rimmed baking sheets lined with parchment paper (you'll be using these to bake the Lahmacun in batches.)
4. Divide the pizza dough into 4 equal balls (about 2 oz each.) Working with one ball of dough at a time, place on a floured surface. Using a rolling pin, roll dough out into as thin as you can to a disk that's about 8 or 9 inches in diameter.
5. Assemble Lahmacun. Place one flat bread disk on one of the prepared pans. Reshape as needed. Spoon 3–4 tbsp topping onto dough and spread topping evenly to edges, leaving a thin boarder.
6. Bake in heated oven for about 5 to 7 minutes or until dough and meat are fully cooked (dough will be a little crusty around the edges.)
7. Repeat steps 5 and 6 with the remaining dough.
8. Squeeze a little lemon juice on top. Serve Lahmacun hot or at room temperature.

Country: Uganda   **Servings: 4**

INGREDIENTS:
- •5 Medium potatoes, peeled and washed
- •6 Large eggs
- •1 C. Bread crumbs
- •1 Tsp. Curry powder
- •1 Tb. Butter/Margarine
- • Pinch of Salt
- • Oil for frying

Ben and Jerry's Ice Cream gets their vanilla from Uganda!

INSTRUCTIONS:
1. Cut the potatoes in half and put them in a pan with enough water to cover the potatoes.
2. Let the potatoes boil till soft and falling apart. 3. Remove from heat and drain the potatoes then set aside to cool.
4. Boil 4 eggs.
5. After the eggs are boiled, remove from heat and let them cool down in cold water.
6. In a bowl, beat the remaining two eggs with a pinch of salt till frothy. Set aside.
7. In another bowl, mash the now slightly cool potatoes. 8. Add the butter, salt and curry and keep mixing till there are no lumps visible.
9. Peel the eggs.
10. Using your hands, gently add the mashed potatoes onto the peeled egg, slowly building your "egg roll" till it is a palm sized ball. Make sure the ball is firm.
11. Gently roll the ball in the whisked egg and then in the breadcrumbs, back into the egg and thoroughly in the bread crumbs. Repeat the process till you have all the rolls ready to fry.
12. Deep-fry the rolls till golden brown.

Country: Ukraine   **Servings: 4**

INGREDIENTS:
- 2 medium size tomatoes
- 4 baby cucumbers
- ½ of small red onion (I've used 1 shallot instead)
- 1-2 garlic cloves
- Fresh dill
- 3 Tbs of sour cream
- 2 Tbs of mayonnaise
- Ground pepper
- Salt to taste

Serve this salad before a main dish. Pairs well with chicken paprikash

INSTRUCTIONS:
1. Prepare ingredients: rinse tomatoes, cucumbers and dill; any kind of cucumbers and tomatoes will work good for this salad, just make sure the ratio of both is more or less the same
2. Start of by preparing dressing. For that put 3 tablespoons of sour cream to a mixing bowl
3. Add about 2 tablespoons of mayonnaise
4. Peel skin from garlic cloves and press it to the bowl
5. Add salt and ground black pepper, mix and set aside
6. Slice tomatoes in wedges into salad bowl
7. If cucumbers are mature and skin is bitter – remove it, cut each cucumber in half lengthwise and slice them
8. Peel and slice onion, add to the bowl
9. Add finely chopped dill
10. Mix everything, add prepared salad dressing and mix again

Country: United Kingdom   **Servings: 4**

INGREDIENTS:
• 3oz dried porcini mushrooms
• 10 Tbs butter
• 2 shallots, finely chopped
• 2 C mixed mushrooms (eg chestnut, oyster, shitaake finely chopped)
• 3 sprigs of thyme, leaves picked
• 7oz Madeira
• 2 Tbs double cream
• 1 Tbs vegetable oil
• 2 lbs beef fillet
• 1 lbs block all-butter puff pastry, plus ½ lb for the lattice
• 1 egg, beaten, to glaze
• 6 slices prosciutto ham

Need a fancy dessert? Pair with Szarlotka on page 124.

INSTRUCTIONS:
1. Preheat the oven, and a flat baking sheet, to 400 DG. Soak the porcini in ¾ C boiling water for 20 minutes, then remove and finely chop. Reserve the soaking water. Melt the butter in a pan over a medium heat and cook the shallots until just golden, then add the mixed mushrooms, porcini and thyme and some salt and pepper and cook until softened. 4.Pour in ¾ C Madeira and turn up the heat, cooking until the wine has evaporated. Take off the heat, and scoop ¾ of the mixture into a bowl. Mix in the double cream, taste for seasoning, and set aside.
2. Heat the oil in a pan over a high heat and, when smoking, add the fillet and sear briefly on all sides until crusted. Season well and allow to cool. Don't wash the pan yet - you'll need it for making the sauce.
3. Roll out the 500 gram block of pastry into rectangles about 11" x 35" and ¼" thick. Brush all over with egg, and then spread with the cream duxelle mixture. Lay the prosciutto ham over the mushrooms and finally place the fillet on top, bending so that it is the shape of a backwards capital J and carefully roll up, finally turning it and positioning it seam-side down. Trim the edges and tuck in to seal the parcel. Using the smaller piece of pastry, cut 0.5 cm wide strips and lay across the, now wellington boot shaped, pastry parcel, in a lattice pattern. Paint with egg and place into the fridge to rest for at least 30 minutes.
4. . When well rested, put the wellington on to the hot baking sheet and cook for 30 minutes until golden, then set aside to rest for 5 minutes. Meanwhile, make the sauce. De glaze the beef pan with the remaining Madeira and then add the remaining mushroom and shallot mixture and the porcini soaking liquid, allowing everything to reduce slightly. Taste, season, and serve with the beef wellington.

Country: Uruguay   **Servings: 4**

INGREDIENTS:
- 4 pieces veal scallopini, thin or veal steaks (or substitute with chicken fillets)
- ½ C flour, all purpose (plain)
- 2 eggs
- salt, ground sea
- black pepper, ground
- Italian herb mix dried
- 1½ C breadcrumbs
- olive oil for shallow frying
- 2 Tbs butter
- 1 lemon cut into wedges

This goes great with the green sauce from Peru!

INSTRUCTIONS:
1. Using a meat mallet, lightly pound the veal until approximately 1/5 of an inch.
2. Sprinkle the flour over a plate. Light beat the eggs, salt, pepper and dried Italian herbs in a shallow bowl. Sprinkle the breadcrumbs on a separate plate.
3. Work with 1 piece of veal at a time. Lightly coat both sides of the veal in the flour, dip into the egg mixture coating both sides and then dip into the breadcrumbs, pressing down lightly with your fingers to ensure breadcrumbs stick to both sides of the veal. Repeat until all veal has been coated and refrigerate for 30 minutes.
4. Pre-heat oven to 200°F. Over a medium heat, add enough olive oil to shallow fry, plus 1 tablespoon of the butter in a heavy pan. When hot, add 2 pieces of veal and cook 2 minutes per side until golden. Drain on kitchen paper and keep warm in the oven while cooking the remaining pieces. Add further oil and remaining butter and cook the remaining pieces.
5. Serve immediately with a wedge of lemon

Country: USA   **Servings: 6**

INGREDIENTS:
- 1 9 inch deep dish pie crust, unbaked
- 1½ C water (that is one and a half cups)
- 4 Tbs all purpose flour
- 1 C sugar
- 2 Tsp vanilla
- 5 Tbs butter, cut into 5 pieces

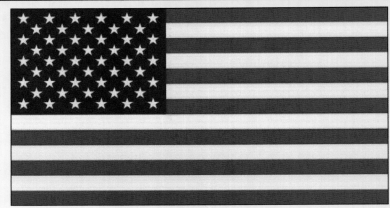

This is a recipe from the Depression Era.

INSTRUCTIONS:
1. Preheat oven to 400°F and set empty pie crust on a baking sheet.
2. Pour 1 + 1/2 cups water into the pie crust.
3. In a small bowl, stir together flour and sugar. Sprinkle evenly over water in crust. Don't stir.
4. Drizzle vanilla over water in pie crust. Place pats of butter on top of this.
5. Bake at 400°F for 30 minutes. Reduce heat to 375 and cover sides of crust if needed to prevent burning. Continue cooking for an additional 30 minutes. 6. Pie will be watery when you pull it out of the oven but will gel as it cools. Allow to cool completely and then cover and place in the fridge until chilled before cutting.

Country: Venezuela   **Servings: 20**

INGREDIENTS:
- 1 C white long grain rice
- 2 C water
- 7 C milk
- 2 cinnamon sticks
- 2 C sugar
- ½ Tsp salt
- 1 Tsp vanilla
- Ground cinnamon to sprinkle

This serves a ton, so cut in half if needed!

INSTRUCTIONS:

1. Wash the rice in flowing water until water comes out clear.

2. In a heavy pot put the water and the rice, bring it to boil and stir for 7 min while cooking until it starts to soften and the water has almost evaporated completely.

3. Add milk and the cinnamon Sticks, bring it to boil and then to medium fire for 15 to 16 minutes until rice soften even more stirring with frequency with a wood spoon

4. Add sugar and cook for another 30 minutes.Add the salt and cook for 1 or 2 more minutes stirring frequently.

5. Take it away from the fire and pour in a glass flat mold, sprinkle some ground cinnamon on the top.

Seared Pork Bánh Mì

SANDWICH INGREDIENTS:
- 6-8 small baguettes
- pickled carrot and radishes (see my note below about making this yourself)
- fresh cilantro, chopped
- 1-2 cucumbers, cut into thin strips
- sliced jalapeños, optional
- Sriracha Mayo
- Pickled Veggies
- Pork

Bánh Mì are typically eaten as a breakfast food

INSTRUCTIONS :

1. Start assembly by slicing baguettes or french rolls. Spread mayo on bottom side of roll.
2. Place several slices of meat over mayo, then layer with a handful of pickled veggies, fresh cucumbers, and fresh cilantro.

Bánh Mì Toppings

PICKLED VEGGIES:
- 10-12 oz. shredded carrots
- 10-12 oz. thin sliced daikon radish or jicama
- 1 C. water
- 1 C. sugar
- 1 C. white vinegar

INSTRUCTIONS:
1. You can buy pickled daikon and carrots or make it yourself. If you make it, you'll want to do this the day before or early in the morning the day of making the sandwiches. It tastes best chilled.
2. To make, boil water with sugar and vinegar. Let boil for 3 minutes to dissolve sugar, then remove from heat.
3. Place sliced veggies into a large mason jar. Once boiled mixture has cooled slightly, pour over veggies in jar. Then close lid tightly and place in fridge for 6-8 hours, or longer.

SIRACHA MAYO:
- ½ mayonnaise
- ½ C sriracha sauce (adjust to how spicy you like it)
- 1 clove garlic, minced
- 1 Tbs. rice vinegar

INSTRUCTIONS:
1. Whisk mayo ingredients together and place in fridge before you make sandwiches. Mayo will taste best when chilled. Adjust levels of sriracha according to how spicy you like it.
2. Leave in fridge until you're ready to assemble sandwiches.

Seared Pork

Pork + Marinade:
- 1½ - 2 lb. pork tenderloin or pork roast no bone
- 1/3 C. fish sauce
- ¼ C. real maple syrup
- 2 Tbs. brown sugar
- ¼ C. soy sauce
- 1 Tsp. sesame oil
- 4 cloves garlic, minced finely
- 2 Tsp. fresh grated ginger
- 2 green onions, sliced thin
- 1 shallot, sliced thin
- 3-4 Tbs. vegetable or canola oil, for cooking meat

INSTRUCTIONS:

1. Before prepping meat, mix marinade ingredients. Mix all marinade ingredients except vegetable/canola oil. Set aside.

2. Start slicing pork roast. Be sure to use a serrated knife so you can get it pretty thin. You want it about 1/4 inch thick. (Not so thin it's falling apart, but not so thick that it will get tough when it cooks.) The pieces will cook down a bit, so make them a little longer and wider than you'd want on a sandwich.

3. Place sliced pork into a heavy duty ziplock bag. Pour marinade on top. Place in fridge for 4-6 hours.

4. Once meat has marinated, remove from fridge. Set out a large pot (I used an enameled dutch oven) and pour about 3 tbsp. of vegetable or canola oil on bottom of pan (enough to cover the bottom about 1/4 inch, depending on your size of pot).

5. Turn heat up to medium high to heat oil. Meanwhile, lay out a large baking sheet lined with paper towels. This will be a great place to set your meat after each batch has cooked in the oil.

6. Once oil has heated, remove pieces of pork one-by-one with tongs from ziplock bag and slowly place into oil (you want oil to sizzle when you place meat in, but if it pops too much, turn heat slightly down).

7. Flip meat over to cook both sides evenly. Once edges start to brown, remove from pot with tongs and set on paper towel lined baking sheet.

8. Sear meat in batches until it's all cooked. Let rest on baking sheet while you assemble the other sandwich ingredients.

Country: Zimbabwe   **Servings: 4 dozen cookies**

INGREDIENTS:
- 10 Tb butter
- ¼ C sugar
- 1 Tb lemon zest
- 1 Tsp ground nutmeg
- ¼ C honey
- 1 egg
- 1 C finely grated raw sweet potato
- 2½ C all-purpose flour
- 1½ Tsp baking powder
- ½ Tsp baking soda
- ½ Tsp salt

Pro tip: grate the sweet potatoes for an even cut.

LEMON GLAZE:
- 1 Tsp butter
- 1-2 Tsp lemon juice
- 1½ C powdered sugar
- 1 Tb water

DIRECTIONS:
1. Cream together butter and sugar in bowl. Blend in lemon zest, nutmeg, honey and egg. Fold in sweet potato.

2. In separate bowl. sift flour, baking powder, baking soda and salt.

3. Add it to the first mixture and blend well. 4. Arrange cookie dough by rounded teaspoons on ungreased cookie sheet. 5. Bake at 350 degrees for 7 minutes. 6. To make glaze, use a wooden spoon to combine all ingredients in glass container until smooth.

7. Add more water by the drop until glaze is easy to spread on cooled cookies.

Bonus Recipes

Country: Afghanistan   **Servings: 6 cups**

Save in the freezer for up to 4 months.

INGREDIENTS:
- 1 large onion, thinly sliced
- 1 stick cinnamon
- 1 black cardamom pod
- 5 black peppercorns
- 5 cloves
- 3 cloves garlic, peeled and grated
- 1 inch ginger, peeled and grated
- 1 Tsp red chili powder
- 1 Tsp coriander powder
- ½ Tsp turmeric
- 3 Thai green chilies
- 3lbs of goats bone (or a whole head) thawed
- 6 C of water (adding more if the broth evaporates more than 3 inches)

INSTRUCTIONS:
1. Slice onion and peel/grate ginger.
2. Add water to a large stock pot and add spices, veggies, and goat bones.
3. Bring to a boil, then reduce to simmer. Simmer for 3-4 hours, adding water if the stock evaporates)
4. Cool and add to soups or drink plain

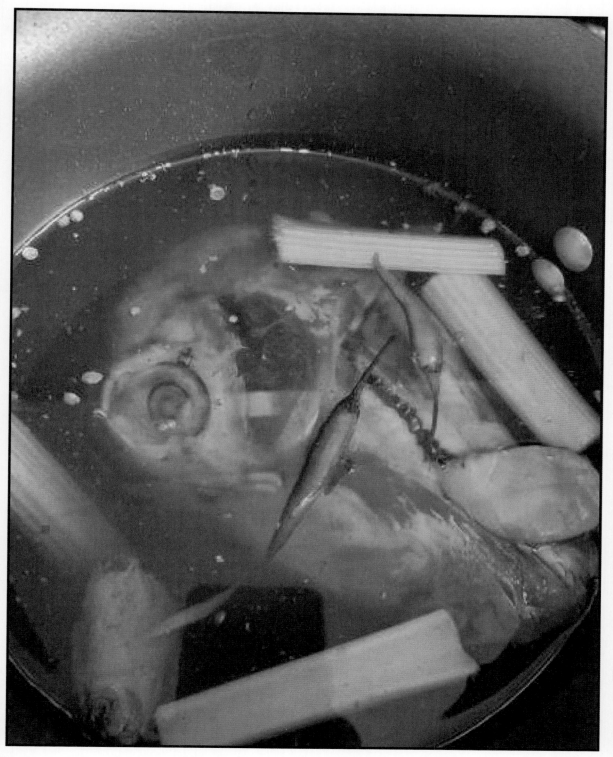

Country: Greece   **Servings: 4 of each**

INGREDIENTS:

Lamb:
- ½ onion, cut into chunks
- 1 pound ground lamb
- 1 pound ground beef
- 1 Tbs minced garlic
- 1 Tsp dried oregano/ ground cumin/ dried marjoram/ ground dried rosemary/ ground dried thyme/ black pepper
- ¼ Tsp sea salt

Chicken:
- 1 lemon juiced
- 1 C plain yogurt
- ½ Tsp salt
- 1 Tsp dried oregano
- 1 Tsp paprika
- 1½ pounds chicken tenders
- 1 Tbs olive oil

INSTRUCTIONS:

Lamb:

1. Place the onion in a food processor, and process until finely chopped. Scoop the onions onto the center of a towel, gather up the ends of the towel, and squeeze out the liquid from the onions. Place the onions into a mixing bowl along with the lamb and beef. Season with the garlic, oregano, cumin, marjoram, rosemary, thyme, black pepper, and salt. Mix well with your hands until well combined. Cover, and refrigerate 1 to 2 hours to allow the flavors to blend.

2. Preheat oven to 325°F.

3. Place the meat mixture into the food processor, and pulse for about a minute until finely chopped and the mixture feels tacky. Pack the meat mixture into a 7x4 inch loaf pan, making sure there are no air pockets. Line a roasting pan with a damp kitchen towel. Place the loaf pan on the towel, inside the roasting pan, and place into the preheated oven. Fill the roasting pan with boiling water to reach halfway up the sides of the loaf pan.

4. Bake until the gyro meat is no longer pink in the center, 45 minutes to 1 hour. Pour off any accumulated fat, and allow to cool slightly before slicing thinly and serving. Fry on both sides for final sear.

Chicken:

1. In a large bowl mix together the lemon juice, plain Greek yogurt, salt, oregano, and paprika. Add the chicken tenders to the marinade and toss to coat. Cover the chicken tenders and transfer the bowl to the refrigerator to marinate for at least 30 minutes to overnight.

2. Heat the olive oil in a large skillet over medium-high heat. Once hot, add the chicken tenders to the skillet (working in batches if necessary). Cook the chicken tenders for 5 minutes, undisturbed, before flipping to the other side to cook for an additional 5-10 minutes more, or until fully cooked.

Bazlama

INGREDIENTS:
- 1¼ C warm water
- 2¼ Tsp active dried yeast
- 1 Tbs sugar
- ¾ C Greek-style yogurt
- 2 Tbs extra virgin olive oil
- 1 Tbs kosher salt
- 3¾ C all-purpose flour
- ¼ C finely chopped flat leaf parsley

This recipe is great for gyros, Lahmacun, or for dipping in curry!

INSTRUCTIONS:

1. Combine the yeast, sugar, and water into a medium-large bowl and stir well. Allow to sit in a warm place for 5-10 minutes to activate the yeast. The mixture will be foamy and bubbly when activated.

2. Whisk in the Greek yogurt olive oil and salt.

3. Add flour and parsley and stir with a wooden spoon or sturdy spatula and until the dough comes together. Turn dough out onto a well-floured counter and turn to coat. Knead for 3-4 minutes or until dough is no longer sticky and springs back when lightly pressed. Sprinkle more flour onto the counter if the dough is sticky during kneading.

4. Divide dough into 10 equal pieces, sprinkle lightly with flour, then cover with a clean kitchen towel. Allow to rest for 15 minutes. 5. Preheat a medium saute pan to a medium-low heat. While pan is heating, roll one of the dough portions into an approximately 7-inch circle. Brush the top surface lightly with extra virgin olive oil. When t the pan is hot, pick up the first circle with your hand and place in pan, oiled side down. Lightly brush the top surface with oil. Allow to the flat bread to cook for about 1 to 1 1/2 minutes, until top surface is covered with bubbles and underside is golden around the edges and in spots.

6. Flip to opposite side and cook for another 60-90 seconds until a few small golden spots appear. Don't overcook on the second side. Repeat rolling, oiling and cooking with remaining portions of dough.

Sago Pearls and Gulaman

INGREDIENTS:

Sago:

- 1 C uncooked sago or tapioca pearls
- 6 C water
- ½ C granulated white sugar

Gulaman

- 1 package (3.1 ounces) unflavored gelatin
- 1 1/2 C water
- 1/4 C sugar

Find tapioca pearls on Amazon or at your local Asian market

INSTRUCTIONS:

Sago:

1. Pour the water in a cooking pot. Let boil.
2. Add-in the sago or tapioca pearls. Cover and boil in medium heat for 30 minutes. Stir every 10 minutes.
3. Put-in the sugar. Stir. Continue to boil for 20 minutes. You can add more water if needed.
4. Turn the heat off. For better results, let the sago or tapioca pearls remain in the cooking pot until it reaches room temperature.

Gulaman:

1. In a pot, combine the package of gelatin, sugar, and 1 1/2 cups water. Whisk together until gelatin is dissolved. Over medium heat, bring to a boil for about 2 to 3 minutes or until mixture begins to bubble. Remove from heat and pour into a baking dish. Refrigerate to cool and set.

Makes 12 servings

INGREDIENTS:
- 1/2 cup minced shallots (about 2 1/2 ounces)
- 1/4 cup white vinegar
- 1/4 cup clear, unseasoned rice vinegar*
- 1/8 teaspoon of sugar
- 1/8 teaspoon of salt
- 1 1/4 teaspoon of finely crushed white peppercorns (do not use pre-ground or powdered white pepper)

The mignonette will last up to a month in the refrigerator.

INSTRUCTIONS:

1. Peel and coarsely chop the shallots. Put them into a food processor and pulse a few times, until the shallots are finely minced. You can also finely mince by hand if you wish, the food processor bowl captures all of the liquid released by the shallots as they are minced, which will enhance the flavor of the mignonette.

2. Place the minced shallots and any liquid released from them in a non-reactive (glass or pyrex) bowl. Add the white vinegar, rice vinegar, and sugar and salt. Stir with a fork. Add the freshly crushed white pepper. Stir with a fork.

3. Cover with plastic wrap and chill in the refrigerator for a minimum of four hours. For best results, store for at least 2 days before using.

The mignonette flavor will be better blended the longer it sits. You may notice that the crushed white peppercorns may sink to the bottom of the bowl as the mignonette rests. If you see this, just give it a little stir.

References

Afghanistan: https://food52.com/recipes/25731-aloo-gosht-pakistani-beef-and-potatostew

Argentina: http://www.tarasmulticulturaltable.com/fugazzeta-argentinian-stuffed-pizza/

Australia: http://petersfoodadventures.com/2015/12/18/honey-joys/

Bahamas: https://www.goodhousekeeping.com/food-recipes/amp11209/bahama-penneseared-mahi-mahi-recipe-df0911/

Bolivia: http://www.food.com/recipe/arroz-con-queso-rice-with-cheese-bolivia-478189

Brazil: https://tasty.co/recipe/classic-brigadeiros

Bulgaria: https://www.geniuskitchen.com/recipe/simple-bulgarian-banitsa-501743

Burma: http://www.196flavors.com/2013/07/17/burma-sanwin-makin/

Cambodia: http://www.malaysianchinesekitchen.com/jackfruit-sago-dessert/

Canada: https://www.fusioncraftiness.com/easy-poutine-recipe/

Chile: https://www.enmicocinahoy.cl/country-chilean-bread/

China: https://www.finecooking.com/recipe/chinese-pork-and-shrimp-dumplings-jiao-zi

Columbia: https://www.cocoandash.com/easy-guava-pastries-guayaba-pastelitos/#wprmrecipe-container-2499

Costa Rica: http://www.angsarap.net/2015/08/17/picadillo-de-chayote/

Croatia : https://wanderlustinthecity.com/2015/07/26/croatian-feta-olive-oil-dip/amp/

Cuba: https://www.lemonblossoms.com/blog/slow-cooker-cuban-mojo-pork/

Denmark: https://www.internationalcuisine.com/dutch-boerenkool-stamppot/

Dominican Republic: http://www.cookitgirl.com/uncategorized/dulce-de-platano-madurocaramelized-sweet-plantains/

Ecuador: https://www.thespruce.com/ecuadorian-fried-cheese-empanadas-3029670?utm_source=pinterest&utm_medium=social&utm_campaign=shareurlbuttons

Egypt: https://www.yummly.com/recipe/Egyptian-Sweet-Cookies-1977976

El Salvador: http://www.sustainingthepowers.com/bean-and-cheese-pupusas-meal-planmonday-7/

Ethiopia: http://www.africanbites.com/ethiopian-cabbage/

Fiji: http://www.thetraveltester.com/banana-cake-recipe-fiji/

Finland: http://cookingtheglobe.com/finnish-salmon-soup-lohikeitto/

France: https://www.halfbakedharvest.com/healthier-instant-pot-coq-au-vin/

Germany: https://www.savorynothings.com/jagerspatzle-german-dumplings-withmushrooms/

Greece: https://theforkedspoon.com/easy-chicken-gyros/

Guatemala: https://www.goya.com/en/recipes/guatemalan-chicken-in-coconut-milk

Honduras: https://therecipeisland.blog/yuca-cake/

Hungary: https://www.allrecipes.com/recipe/140555/chicken-paprikash/?utm_source=pinterest.com&utm_medium=social&utm_campaign=allrecipes_allrecipes_66 86097&utm_content=worldcuisine_video&utm_term=global_201902

Iceland: https://www.internationalcuisine.com/icelandic-caramelized-potatoes/

India: https://healthiersteps.com/recipe/instant-pot-vegan-jackfruit-with-potato-curry/

Indonesia: https://www.tastemade.com/videos/indonesian-coconut-pancake

Iran: http://www.thedeliciouscrescent.com/persian-lubia-polo/

Israel: http://thefitchen.com/2016/10/26/howtocookisraelicouscous/

Italy: https://www.biggerbolderbaking.com/easy-10-minute-tiramisu/

Jamaica: http://serenityfood.com/jamaican-oxtail/

Japan: https://www.thespruceeats.com/tempura-batter-recipe-2031529?
utm_source=pinterest&utm_medium=social&utm_campaign=mobilesharebutton2

Laos: http://seonkyounglongest.com/larb-laap-laab/

Latvia: https://bellyrumbles.com/piragi-latvian-bacon-buns/

Libya: https://www.internationalcuisine.com/libyan-bread/

Madagascar: http://www.internationalcuisine.com/malagasy-mofo-sakay/

Malaysia: http://www.wandercooks.com/ridiculously-fun-malaysian-teh-tarik/

Marshall Island: https://www.internationalcuisine.com/marshallese-chukuchuk/

Mexico: http://www.bettycrocker.com/recipes/chocoflan/
907b4e0d-9604-467c-8c3ed95536b5a51b?
nicam4=SocialMedia&nichn4=Pinterest&niseg4=BettyCrocker&nicreatID4=Post&crlt.pid=c
amp.qua3SOdGBF7n

Morocco: http://www.sainsburysmagazine.co.uk/recipes/mains/item/moroccan-chickenflatbreads

Nepal: http://www.food.com/recipe/chicken-sekuwa-classic-nepali-chicken-skewers-86984

Netherlands: http://tarasmulticulturaltable.com/gulerodsbrud-danish-carrot-rolls/

New Zealand: https://www.thehomecookskitchen.com/best-pavlova-recipe/?
utm_medium=social&utm_source=pinterest&utm_campaign=tailwind_tribes&utm_content
=tribes&utm_term=585099192_20213600_436296

Nicaragua: https://www.casablancacooks.com/gallo-pinto/

Nigeria: https://feelgoodfoodie.net/recipe/west-african-beef-kabobs/

Norway: https://kitchendreaming.com/noregian-kjottkaker-meatballs/

Pakistan: https://food52.com/recipes/25731-aloo-gosht-pakistani-beef-and-potato-stew

Panama: https://www.buzzfeed.com/JCGibbsDC/15-panamanian-dishes-you-must-trybbet

Peru: http://tastyfoodvideos.com/

Philippines: https://www.kawalingpinoy.com/sago-at-gulaman/

Poland: http://www.costcodiva.com/szarlotka-polish-apple-cake/

Portugal: https://portugueserecipes.ca/recipe/1001/23/

Portuguese-Creamy-ChickenSteaks-Recipe

Romania: http://honestcooking.com/kurtoskalacs-chimney-cake/

Russia: https://www.mrfood.com/Beef/russian-piroshki-101

Samoa: https://momfoodie.com/pani-popo-3-ingredient-samoan-coconut-rolls/

Serbia: http://www.tarasmulticulturaltable.com/musaka-serbian-potato-moussaka/

Singapore: http://linsfood.com/chilli-crab/

South Africa: https://multiculturalcookingnetwork.wordpress.com/2013/12/06/southafrican-tripe-recipe-a-favorite-of-nelson-mandelas/

South Korea: http://seonkyounglongest.com/beef-hot-pot/

Spain: http://www.melaniecooks.com/easy-spanish-paella-recipe-how-to-make-paellain-30-minutes/9068/

Switzerland: http://laurencariscooks.com/traditional-swiss-cheese-fondue/

Taiwan: https://therecipecritic.com/slow-cooker-mongolian-beef/

Thailand: http://houseofnasheats.com/thai-coconut-mango-sticky-rice/

Turkey: https://www.themediterraneandish.com/easy-turkish-lahmacun-recipe/

Uganda: https://akitcheninuganda.com/2016/05/17/how-to-make-a-ugandan-eggroll/

Ukraine: http://www.enjoyyourcooking.com/salads/ukrainian-tomato-cucumbersourcream.html

United Kingdom: https://www.tastemade.co.uk/videos/boot-beef-wellington

Uruguay: http://www.compassandfork.com/recipe/make-uruguays-golden-veal-milanesa/

USA: https://www.southernplate.com/water-pie-recipe-from-the-great-depression/

Venezuela: http://recipes.sparkpeople.com/recipe-detail.asp?recipe=169236

Vietnam: http://plumstreetcollective.com/seared-pork-bahn-mi/

Zimbabwe: http://www.food.com/recipe/cookies-from-zimbabwe-139868

Index

Sides:

Desserts:

Breads:

Drinks:

Bonus recipes: